Gratefully Looking Back
A Doctor's Special Journey

Biography, Autobiography, Memoirs Series

Rudolf H. Bock

Gratefully Looking Back
A Doctor's Special Journey

ARIADNE PRESS
Riverside, California

Library of Congress Cataloging-in-Publication Data

Bock, Rudolf H., 1915 April 20 -
    Gratefully looking back : a doctor's special journey / Rudolf H. Bock.
        p.   cm. -- (Studies in Austrian literature, culture and thought.
    Biography, autobiography, memoirs series)
    ISBN 1-57241-110-4
    1. Bock, Rudolf H., 1915 April 20 2. Jewish physicians--Austria--Biography.
    3. Holocaust, Jewish (1939-1945)--Personal narratives. 4. Antisemitism--Austria.
    5. Jews--Austria--Biography. I. Title. II. Series.

R694 .B63 2002
610'.92--dc21
[B]   2002074633

Cover Design:
Art Director, Designer: George McGinnis
Photo: Hedda Hammer

Contents

Acknowledgments

I would like to acknowledge the following people who have assisted, encouraged and supported me in writing my autobiography.

The Rev. Dr. Alfred Williams for his initial encouragement, Ellen Brigham and Gloria Freed M.D. for their editorial comments and Dr. Joseph Adler for his ongoing support and putting it all together.

Rudolf Bock in Peking, 1939

Early Life in Austria

Christmas eve, 1975 – a good day to start what I have been planning now for several weeks – namely to put to paper some of the events of my early life. Having lived away from home now for almost two months, I am more acutely aware of the importance of my relationship with my children, grown as they may be, and writing this narrative for them makes me feel good. In spite of everything, I still do believe that I have a family and that some day they may be interested enough to read this story. I wish my father had left us some documents of his life experiences. I always regretted that we knew so little about him.

So let me start with what little I do remember about him. He was a quiet, retiring and soft-spoken man, always around, but never much noticed. I know that he was very attached to his family and our home life, in which my mother, definitely the leading figure, was very peaceful. I don't recall a single instance of a quarrel or harsh words between my parents. If they had differences, they never showed them and they seemed quietly devoted to each other. They had first met when my mother, aged fourteen, took an art class with this "good looking teacher" – he was then thirty-one. He was always hard working, conscientious and probably quite enterprising in his youth. I assume this from the fact that he did visit Mama once in Wiener Neustadt before they got married in 1909, coming from Vienna on a motorcycle. I don't think motorcycles were very commonplace in those days. This story was remembered because he apparently had a minor accident on the way and arrived with completely torn pants!

He did his share of mountain travel, and I specifically

remember picture postcards of the Ortler Gruppe in South Tyrol, where he walked with a friend over a high pass (Stilfser Joch). He always loved to walk, and I often joined him on his regular Sunday morning strolls through the fields around Wiener Neustadt, which he took until the very last years. On these walks we would, naturally, communicate, but I don't remember discussing more than ordinary, everyday problems of practical living or subjects of our immediate surroundings. There did not seem to be any major problems, we children had no obvious growing-up pains to speak of. We all did well in school and were healthy. And there wasn't the exaggerated generation gap or the crime, unrest and insecurity of our present day society. I liked to be with him even if there were no important matters to be discussed.

For the last twenty years of his active life, he was principal of the School of Business in Wiener Neustadt, an industrial town of about 40,000 inhabitants, thirty-five miles south of Vienna. We moved there from Vienna when I was five years old. Teachers were very poorly paid; his salary was modest, but somehow we were always well taken care of because of his careful budgeting (after all, the main subject he taught was accounting). I still remember how he had made hard paper envelopes for Mama's bookkeeping, so that she could keep the various items clearly separated. At the first of each month when he brought home his salary, the amount allocated for each item was placed in these envelopes. There was always the envelope for education for us and one for summer vacation. The latter seemed very important to us children, because it meant that we could look forward to our two months summer vacation at Attersee (a beautiful lake near Salzburg).

Papa had several hobbies. He loved to work with wood and made some beautiful pieces in jigsaw work and woodcarving.

We had no power tools in those days, of course, and his tool box was rather small but carefully guarded with everything kept in perfect condition. It was a great honor and sign of trust when he first allowed me to use his tools. What a different situation it was with my children! No wonder I always got mad when they used my tools without my permission and messed them up – my childhood memories were violated! When I see my son Michael nowadays in his workshop, with all his fancy tools in fine order and condition, I often think of my father and how he would have enjoyed watching his grandson and be proud of him.

His two other great hobbies were fishing and mushroom hunting, but he could indulge in these only during our vacation on the lake. What I know about these two subjects, I learned from him. I loved to sit with him in our boat or on the pier to catch fish, or walk with him through the wet woods in search of edible mushrooms. I never took up fishing (I always felt sorry for the poor creatures), but I still like mushroom hunting and took it up again when we were in Arcata two years ago. So far we have never been poisoned.

My father's pride and joy was our rowboat, named KURU after us boys Kurt and Rudi (no Li for Lislott was added when my sister was born). He used it not only for fishing, but we also made many long exploratory trips rowing along the shores and across the lake. Attersee is the largest of the Salzkammergut lakes, about thirteen miles long and one and a half miles wide with hilly shores on the north end and steep high mountains (Schafberg, Hoellengebirge) in the south. On those trips, my place as a little boy was usually at the bow. I liked to lie prone on the front seat and drag my hands in the water, wondering what was going on in the mysterious depths or watching the little waves made by the tip of the boat. Mama used to sit at the stern, steering while Papa and Kurt were rowing – a rather typical distribution of roles and characters in our family!

Even though we stayed at various villages around the lake in the many summers we spent there, it was always the same lake, only seen from a different shore. This gave us a special intimate feeling for the area. I remember how excited I always was when our slow train, eight to ten hours after leaving Vienna, approached the area. (It takes three and a half hours by car today on the freeway.) One could see the characteristic outlines of the Schafberg from far away and the nearer we came, the more familiar the features appeared. It was a delightful homecoming. Even in my later life when I passed by that area by train, car or plane, I searched the topography for familiar landmarks with a deep feeling of nostalgia.

And there are very good reasons for that – happy childhood memories! The earliest memory, however, which I don't actually remember and which was not exactly happy, dates back to the age of fourteen months. I had just learned to walk and Mama had left me by myself for a moment in the front yard of the house we were renting while she went into the kitchen. The yard, bordering on the lake, was well fenced off, but it had a little gate to the step down to the boat landing and pier. This gate was usually locked, but Mama had forgotten to check it and, naturally, that is where I went. When she looked out the kitchen window a few moments later, she didn't see me in the yard and saw the gate open. She rushed out and, finding me floating under water below the pier, pulled me out and gave me my life for the second time. I guess a psychiatrist might deduce something from this event.

I have particularly happy memories of one summer when I

was about ten years old and we were staying at the house of the Ericher family, who were the fishermen of the tiny hamlet, Parschallen. We had invited two other young boys along as guests. They were brothers and the older one was Kurt's classmate in High School (Gymnasium). They both were full of fun and mischief and we had a great time together. The Erichers had two sons of their own, the older one, Franzl, about eighteen years old and the younger one, Hansl, about my age. Franzl was already helping his father with the fishing, going out every morning long before sunrise to bring in the catch and then, after taking care of the fish, repairing for hours on end the torn nets with their intricate knots. I never tired of watching. I came to consider Hansl my special friend. The two of us used to catch butterflies together, a hobby I had started the year before (and never quite abandoned till now). These were happy hunting days (not for the butterflies) and I got to know every bush and tree in the area.

I said that I considered Hansl my special friend because 1 still remember how 1 tried to keep up a correspondence with him (mostly about butterflies) after we came back from summer vacation. I kept a little diary in which I recorded every day, "No answer yet from Hansl." Eventually I got tired of this same stupid phrase and just wrote the first letter of each of these 5 words. I continued this for several weeks before giving up. Anyway, while we were in Parschallen, our gang had a very happy time. There was a little creek coming down alongside the Erichers' house. It had been dammed up to supply the water power for a nearby abandoned saw mill. Fishing just below the dam was very good. We also had lots of fun with the huge water wheel when playing various games of chase. Where the creek entered the lake in a delta-like gravel bed was the best place to catch little fish that hid behind the rocks. Franzl was an expert in doing this with his bare hands and since we children were not as successful, we always pestered him to catch them for us. In that same place, there also were beautifully polished pebbles that would break into many pieces along sharp interfaces when knocked against a hard object. They made ideal puzzles when trying to reassemble them. Marvelous for rainy days – and there were many of those in the Salzkammergut!

Some years our grandparents (Mama's parents – Leopold and Irma Patek) would come and stay with us for a few weeks. They had always lived in Wiener Neustadt where my grandfather had a tobacco store. He was a very kind, but quite emotional man who could fly into a rage easily, but never for a long time. I still remember my first encounter with him when we moved from Vienna to Wiener Neustadt. He came to Vienna to take me down with him a few days before my parents and Kurt followed with the moving van. I felt very lonely away from my family for the first time and also missed my toys, especially my toy train. I must have made a lot of fuss about that, for one morning when I woke up, there was my little train next to my bed. My grandfather had gone to Vienna again to bring it to me. I thought this was very nice of him – and I shall never forget it.

Since I am back at my early childhood, I might as well insert a few memories from that time. The earliest thing that I can recall from Vienna was an outing in the Gartengasse (where I was born and where we lived at #19 A on the third floor). Apparently I had insisted on being taken in the stroller even though I could walk very well already. We met an acquaintance who looked at me with surprise and said to Mama, "But he shouldn't be in a stroller anymore!" I felt so ashamed of myself for having played baby. There was another young couple, the Forsters, living in the identical apartment just above us. They also had two boys about our age. We children always played together and even had a string elevator going from their children's room windows down to ours, to send toys or food up and down. At that time I was crazy about bottles, the smaller they were, the better I liked them. I had quite a collection because friends always brought me some. Usually about once a week I would go up to the Forsters, ring the bell and say, "Stör ich?" (Am I welcome?), and then "Do you have any bottles for me? I never lived down the "Stör ich." They always teased me about it – and all I had done was to be polite and repeat what Mama had told me to say.

I was about six or seven when I got interested in a toy sailboat that I had always admired in a show window on my way to school. My birthday was coming up and I told Mama about this boat. She got the hint and took me to the store to buy the boat. They had them in all sizes and colors so it was hard to decide which one to get. In my deeply ingrained modesty, I chose a rather small one while longingly eyeing a larger and prettier one. Mama must have noticed what was going on inside me and said, "It is your birthday, so let's get the bigger one!" I never forgot this lesson, maybe because it contradicted the usual pattern expressed by Wilhelm Busch, "Bescheidenheit ist eine Zier, doch weiter kommt man ohne ihr." (Modesty is honorable, but you get farther without it.)

It was at Attersee that I got to know Uncle Paul better. He is Mama's younger brother, and since he was never married and did not have children of his own, he liked to do things with us and for us. He always was a little bit of a nut, very imaginative and funny, a great actor, a gifted pianist and cellist, and a good writer and sculptor. I started playing the cello on his instrument at the age of sixteen. How many happy hours have I had with it! In his later years he developed the hobby of weaving carpets and both Kurt and I have several of these. Paul had not been a very good student – he probably was too naughty as a boy. He actually flunked in Gymnasium and instead went to a Technical High School. Right after graduation, he was drafted into the Austrian army with the outbreak of the first World War in 1914 and fought on the Italian front for four years. The story goes that when he had to leave for the front, he bought a monkey for his mother "to replace him." I still remember the large cage in which the animal was kept up in their attic. Wherever he went during the war, he always had his dog along. Dogs remained his best companions throughout his life.

After the war, he worked in a locomotive factory, learning all about forging metal, but then he went into private business selling safety locks, which was more lucrative and exciting. In this work his talents as an actor could be deployed to their fullest. Paul suffered all his life from his homosexual inclination, since people in Austria were far from enlightened in this matter. For the greater part of his adult life he lived with his friend, Carl, whom we all, except Papa, liked very much. Papa had a strong prejudice when it came to this subject and did not want to have anything to do with him. When I was old enough to know about Paul and Carl's relationship, I could never quite understand my father's uncompromising attitude. I knew that, as a person, he had nothing against Paul and he might have overlooked the matter for Mama's sake, but he couldn't. The time Paul visited with us at Attersee, Carl was not in the picture yet. Paul loved sailing, which is a very favorite sport on this big lake with its ideal wind conditions. Whenever he came, he rented a sailboat and took us along, racing over the waves. That was more fun than our little rowboat, but could be really scary, too. Paul was very generous, and his presents to us at Christmas time were always the most exciting and original ones. It was really too bad that Papa had such strong, negative feelings. In retrospect, they may have played a large role in Papa's decision not to follow Paul's invitation to all the family to join him in Japan when we had to leave Austria after the annexation by the Nazis in 1938.

When I was fifteen (and Kurt was twenty), we decided to reach Attersee by bicycle and join our parents and Lislott there for the summer vacation. Naturally we chose the more scenic road that went over Semmering Pass, Leoben, Prebichl Pass, Gesaeuse, Hallstaetter See and Ischl and not the more or less flat northern route via Vienna. In those days there were no ten-speed bikes and practically no paved roads. Fortunately, there were also very few cars, because each one left us in a huge cloud of dust for about five minutes. Another major nuisance was the prevailing west wind, which slowed us down considerably. All the uphill stretches we had to walk and push the bikes with their heavy rucksacks on the rack. We made it up on the ordinary downhill runs except down the very steep Prebichl Pass. It was so cold that we had to put socks on our hands (we had no gloves) to prevent them from freezing to the brake handles. We needed large branches tied to the bikes and dragged behind us to slow us down – the coaster brakes simply could not handle it. There were many unforgettable scenes and we probably never laughed as much together as on this trip.

In Bruck a Mur we found, after a long search, a cheap hotel room (our budget was extremely limited) and slept soundly until about midnight when we both woke up itching all over. The cause was easily discovered – bedbugs all over the sheets, all sizes and all colors and then the telltale brown lines on the walls where previous visitors had executed those lovely little insects. We should have noticed these before renting the room! We also should have seen the large can of Flit, a well-known pesticide, under the staircase as we came up. By flashlight, we killed as many bugs as we could find, but they kept coming and didn't give us any peace. Finally I moved my blanket onto the floor. It was hard, but at least no bites. We did not sleep too much that night and decided to stay away from this kind of accommodation thereafter, so we spent the next night in a hayloft. It looked like a nice place and the farmer who gave us permission to spend the night there was very friendly. We had overlooked the fact that our loft was over the stables and we learned to our dismay that cows, chewing their cud all night long, can be very noisy. So we gradually learned our lessons, enjoyed the beautiful scenery all along the way and generally had a very good time. This one week brought us even closer together than we had already been.

Kurt has always been more than an ordinary brother to me and whatever dependency relationships I may have had in my life, the one with him will be the last one I'll outgrow, if I ever will do so. We are very different, but somehow complement each other and can relate to one another with complete and utter trust and openness. He is much more this-worldly and practical than I. In many ways he, in his natural and deep concern for us all, replaced or supplemented Papa, particularly for my sister Lislott, who was exceptionally close to him. He shared all his problems and ideas with Mama till her final days and this relationship was, for her, the most important thing in her life after we lost Papa in 1941. As far as I can know, I never resented in the least that Mama seemed to be closer to Kurt than to her two other children. It was an accepted fact. I just thought that he was an exceptionally good son and wished I, myself, had more of an emotional attachment to my mother. All these subtle trends were never a problem to me until they were pointed out to me by my wife, Trude, who saw them from her viewpoint – maybe more objectively – or maybe not.

I have never known my grandparents on my father's side. They apparently did not live together in their later life. Mama met my grandmother, Katarina, only a few times. My grandfather, Albert, had been a real estate broker. There were five children, two boys and three girls. We got to know two of my father's sisters, Rosa and Anna, very well and liked them. The third sister, Paula, was married to a cousin in Bangkok. His one brother, Sam, acted as my guide when, at the age of fourteen, I went to Vienna for the first time alone to visit the Museum of Natural History – to see, of course, the butterfly collection. My grandmother, Katarina, still practiced the Jewish religion. Mama recalled that Katarina was very upset when my parents converted to Catholicism soon after they got married. Papa retained nothing of his Jewish heritage except to light a candle on the aniverary of his father's death and to eat matzo at Easter time. Neither did he practice Catholicism. I never saw him enter a church and he was not even present at my first communion. Religion was never mentioned in our house. Papa was an outspoken socialist and, as such, on political grounds did not feel warmly towards the "Schwarzen" (the Catholic party).

Around the turn of the century, there was a strong trend toward assimilation of the Jewish minority by conversion to Christianity and intermarriage. In the pre-Hitler Austria, conversion to Catholicism practically removed all discriminatory obstacles that Jews had to face at every turn. Austria was, and still is, an anti-Semitic country. I have never asked my parents why they converted, but I am sure it was partly because they thought it would make our (the children's) lives easier. I remember the story that my father told about his interview with the mayor of Vienna. In his earlier years, as a public school teacher, he had been denied promotion and, therefore, joined a private school that accepted Jewish teachers. Before leaving the public school system, however, he appealed the denial of promotion and his dossier went all the way up to the mayor. For some reason, the good man had not studied his dossier carefully when Papa appeared for the interview. When he leafed through it and saw all the excellent qualifications my father had, he was quite puzzled, until he noticed the entry "Religion – Jewish." "Oh, I see!" he muttered under his breath and Papa knew what he meant. After the first World War, when Austria had a socialist government, anti-Semitism was much less obvious. He had no problem when he applied in 1920 for the position of Director of the city sponsored School of Business in Wiener Neustadt. It helped, though, that my Uncle Victor, his sister Rosa's husband, who was a socialist congressman, put in a word for him at the socialist controlled city council!

Until the Nazis came to power in Austria in 1938, we as a family were not really affected by anti-Semitism – we were baptized and accepted. Mama had converted to Catholicism under the influence of her best friend, Aunt Gretl, who was an impressive lady in her straightforwardness and sincerity. She would have made a good modern liberal Catholic in this country. Mama did not practice her Catholicism either, so all the religious education that we children got was from school. It was a very traditional Catholicism, certainly not very intellectual as one would expect it to be in a High School curriculum. It became more a training of memory than an understanding of the essence, significance or history of Christianity. We never read the Bible, only learned the names of the books in their right order by heart. There was no mention of the fact that Christianity evolved out of Judaism and the modern term Judeo-Christian tradition might have sounded blasphemous. I often wish that we had gotten more acquainted with the Jewish tradition, but our parents made no effort in that direction since they did not practice it themselves and probably did not believe in it.

I was a pious little boy, enjoying the awe and mystery connected with everything that had to do with the church. First communion was a big social event, and I remember being dressed in my best clothes and walking up to the altar with all the other eight-year-olds, and the big cake feast following. I also remember, later on, singing in the choir in a Schubert Mass. I loved the music, and the text, "Wohin soll ich mich wenden, wen Gram und Schmerz mich drücken ...." (Where can I turn when worry and pain depress me ....) is still with me. I liked to go into churches to admire the architecture and to feel the mysterious power and quiet that makes one turn inward and upward and away from the hassles of daily life outside. There frequently is an intimacy and peacefulness in many of the small empty village churches that can't be equaled by anything – I love them.

When I was about thirteen, some critical thoughts began to spring up and things changed. I began to feel funny about having to dream up little sins, like stealing pencils etc., in order to have something to say when I went to confession. Many of the dogmas and rules didn't seem to make too much sense. Gradually the emotional involvement weakened and my intellect developed and seemed to promise better answers to unanswerable questions.

I was very fond of animals as a young boy. One block from our flat was the huge park of the old Military Academy, originally founded by the Empress Maria Theresa (around 1780). Parts of it were almost wilderness. There were ponds and even a river running through it; it was an inviting place to observe animal life. I had several little friends, Willy among them, with similar inclinations. In the springtime we used to roam all through the woods to find bird's nests and to watch the baby birds grow up. Once I even found a young falcon that had fallen out of the nest and was obviously abandoned by its mother. I took it home and tried to raise it on raw liver, which was quite a chore because the little fellow was always hungry and was continuously screeching for more food. It was fun to see him develop his permanent plumage, but I was relieved when he finally was ready to fly off. We made all kinds of traps to catch birds and squirrels, but never succeeded, fortunately. Once I found a hedgehog that I tried to have as a pet for a while, but he did not like the confinement of our flat and refused to eat what I had to offer. Field mice did a little better and I loved to watch their shiny black eyes. The most successful survivors were small salamanders that we caught in ponds. The dark gray males looked like tiny dragons with their impressive dorsal comb. The females were less showy – more like our newts, in a smaller form. It was fun to watch them lay eggs!

I always was interested in watching animals; but my little friends, in particular Willy, had a strong hunting instinct and at times we all carried slingshots. On one of these hunting expeditions, Willy hit a large bird. I saw it dropping down and struggling, then eventually dying. I got very upset – had we really intended to kill that bird? A little later, on the same outing, I was hit in my eye by a little rock projectile bouncing off a tree trunk. It must have caused a corneal erosion because it was excruciatingly painful and my eye watered so profusely that I could not see anything. My first thought was of the bird we had killed and this made me feel even worse. The boys led me home and Mama took me to our eye doctor. I decided that was it! No more slingshots!

Our High School, which was a "progressive" eight-year, state sponsored, boarding school for boys, was housed in the old Military Academy buildings. Actually it was the twelfth century castle of the Babenberger dynasty. Maria Theresa had enlarged and modernized the castle 150 years previously, an enormous rectangular complex with a large central courtyard. Our classrooms and dorms were huge and there were also quite a few hidden, often underground, passages and cellars to be explored. Some of these must have served as prison cells centuries ago. One could let one's imagination run wild while finding broken pottery pieces and even human skeletal bones in some of these dark dungeons. Our students came from all parts of the country and we were a lively bunch, not much concerned with the spooky Middle Ages. We formed a rather closely knit community of which I felt very much a part even though I was not a boarder, but lived at home a block away.

Where I really loved to go was the deciduous forest along the river Leitha, the "Au," which was about half an hour from home. One rarely met anyone there, except on weekends in early spring when people would come to look for the first wildflowers – snowbells, primulas, etc. I enjoyed racing on my bike on the narrow paths. I knew every turn and bump, the branches hitting me when I passed through a narrow passage. Then I would lie in the meadows along the river, watching the birds and other animals around me. Other times I went after butterflies and caterpillars. I specifically remember one early Sunday morning when I rode out there to retrieve my pocket knife, which I had forgotten the day before while studying at my favorite spot. I found it and sat down to rest a little. The place looked enchanted with the fresh dew drops on the leaves and on a spider web in front of me glistening in the sun. Small humming insects were all around me, appearing here and there as they lit up in a sun ray that filtered through the trees. I myself sat in a sunny spot, leaning relaxed against a tree and felt very much at ease and at peace with myself and my surroundings. Suddenly it occurred to me that I was not an intruder in this little world of plants and animals, but somehow a part of it all. It was the kind of feeling that I believe St. Francis may have had when he talked of his "brother" or "sister" in referring to things in nature – a sense of closeness, of being akin to all creatures, as opposed to our common, purely human-oriented point of view.

It was not until I was sixteen that I became rudely aware of my Jewish background. A classmate told me one day that my mother's parents were Jewish. It was an awful shock to me, but the identity crisis did not last too long. We talked things over at home and I matured a few years in a few hours. Hitler was not yet in power in Germany, but his vicious anti-Semitic doctrines were spreading into Austria, kindling old dormant feelings there. Who could anticipate that they would soon break out into open flames that eventually would lead to the holocaust?

While the forces of evil under Hitler were struggling up to power, there were many more constructive ideas around that worked for understanding among the nations of Europe. One of these was student exchange programs. My parents arranged for both Kurt and me to take part in them. Kurt went to England in 1930 and I to France (Albertville on the Isère) in 1931. I had had seven years of French in High School by then, but my conversational French was very poor and this was an excellent way to develop it. It was the first time that I left my home country, so I was somewhat apprehensive, but Kurt encouraged me, backed up by his good experiences the year before.

On the way through Switzerland, I stopped in Zurich to stay for a few days with Siegfried and Anne Herzog, Mama's cousins. They had four sons, all older than I. One of them, Hans, was a detail man for a Swiss pharmaceutical firm and traveled a great deal. I came just at the right time when he had a trip planned to Luzern, Bern and Basel, so I got to see a lot of this beautiful country, I was particularly impressed by Luzern and the Vierwaldstaetter See. Schiller's William Tell play comes to mind immediately when one sees this scenery where it supposedly happened. One can understand why these mountain people loved their home country to the point that they were willing to rebel against their feudal overlord. That is where the feudal system first began to crack and freedom to win. What is surprising is that this tradition has been kept alive now for over 700 years.

My Uncle Siegfried was originally from Austria, where he had studied engineering, but had left Austria after experiencing unpleasant anti-Semitic tendencies among the students there. He took a job with Brown-Bovery, the largest Swiss electromechanical company, and succeeded rapidly, unimpeded by racial prejudice. Eventually he went into private consulting work, allowing him more time for his hobby, which was painting. He loved to copy famous canvases. When I was there, he worked on a painting by Defregger, the Tirolean artist, and it took him the better part of three days to finish one little finger. I sat by him quite a bit of the time and learned the technique of oil painting. When I left, he presented me with his old watercolor set – but I never mastered that art. Anyway, it was a good stimulus and got me interested in this hobby which I still enjoy very much.

Albertville is a beautiful little town, surrounded by rather high mountains, most of which we climbed during the month I stayed there. My host family consisted only of the mother, Madame Gachet, and her seventeen-year-old son, Jean. She had lost her husband right at the onset of the first World War and Jean had never known his father. It was obvious why Madame Gachet, who had supported herself and raised her son alone was involved in international student exchange. She earned her living as a school teacher and I am sure she was a pretty strict one. With me, she was very kind and patient and seemed delighted with my rapid progress in conversational French, so I felt very much at home with "my" family. The Gachets belonged to the French Alpine Club and we joined the club outings often on weekends. The area is very close to Mont Blanc, and the scenery was superb. I developed the habit of collecting memorial rocks from each peak that I climbed. I also collected interesting ones from along the way, like the beautiful quartz crystals on Grand Mont. Some of these I even took with me to China. The second half of the summer Jean spent with us in Austria. I think he enjoyed himself as much as I did in Albertville but, for some reason, we did not keep up a correspondence for long thereafter. I corresponded for years with his mother, though.

It was during this time also that I became interested in philosophy, mainly through Schopenhauer. I don't know why this pessimist's writings fascinated me. It couldn't be only because he is so readable, which most other German philosophers are not (I still cannot understand Kant, unless I read him in an English translation!). I read Schopenhauer's *Aphorismen zur Lebensweisheit* so many times that some of its passages are still with me. It took me a long time to outgrow his cynical and biased outlook on life, in particular his view on the female sex and anything that has to do with feelings and emotions. He must have had very sad experiences along these lines himself.

23

I guess a modern psychologist would analyze him as the product of a loveless, unhappy childhood. All I know about his mother is that she was a very intellectual woman and a famous writer in her own right. Among the German Classics it was, of course, Goethe that I admired most, and I read his Faust so many times that I know many passages by heart. Every time I read him again in later life, I found new pearls of wisdom in it that had escaped me before because I had not had the personal experience and, therefore, the resonance to understand them. Among the modern writers, Hermann Hesse was in great vogue and I liked him, too.

In school we also read a fair number of the French Classics, like Racine, Corneille and Molière which I didn't mind because we had a very fine French teacher, Dr. Berner. He was my favorite and our class was fortunate to have him as our main "Erzieher" (counselor) through all of our eight years (ten to eighteen years of age). He certainly knew every one of us inside out after this time. After my summer in France, it was no problem for me to pass my graduation finals (Matura) in French, which was one of my majors. I was deeply grieved to see Dr. Berner die of stomach cancer two years after my graduation. I still remember visiting him as a patient in the hospital, emaciated to the bones with sunken but still kind eyes. I tried to comfort him – when he knew better that there was no hope. Apparently, I felt that this was my prerogative because I was by then a medical student and imagined I knew more about life and death than any ordinary person in his last days!

What required the most work for my finals was my optional thesis, which consisted of playing surveyor and drawing a detailed map of a section of the "Hohe Wand." This 700 foot high and four-mile long, reddish limestone cliff is situated about two hours bicycle ride west of Wiener Neustadt, and we went there frequently to practice rock climbing. It was there, at the foot of this cliff, that I saw for the first time in my life a dying person – a rock climber who had fallen off the wall shortly before we passed by. I stayed with the injured man while Kurt ran down to the next village to get help. It was rather ghastly. The man was unconscious, but still moving and groaning, and I didn't know what to do. I did observe that the skin of both lids around the eyes were all dark blue. Later I learned that this "spectacle hematoma" was typical for a fracture of the base of the skull, which is usually fatal. Actually, by the time Kurt came back with help, the man had expired. Why I chose a half-mile section of that cliff for surveying I still don't understand. No wonder that my math teacher, Professor Lipp, under whom I did this project, was always worried to death about our climbing around in those rocks every weekend. But nothing happened. With Kurt's or some classmate's help (it always takes at least two people for surveying), I got all my measurements and had the beautifully colored contour map that spread over two tables ready for the finals. Professor Lipp was so relieved that he gave me an A in math which I certainly did not deserve otherwise. My third major subject was biology and that had never been a problem for me. So I passed with flying colors and was ready for university.

How did I decide to go into medicine? I don't remember that it was such a difficult choice. I was not given to much soul searching in those years – that came later. The only alternative that I considered was geology and surveying, since I liked the outdoors and the mountains. What I had seen of medicine impressed me more. Our family physicians had always been outstandingly nice people (Dr. Gerstl, Dr. Glaser) and, of course, Onkel Rudi, Mama's cousin, had tried to steer me in that direction. He had a good OB GYN practice in Vienna and was happy in his profession, even though he was a terrible pessimist in his general outlook on life. I always thought it must be nice to be able to help people when they were in need. In what other profession can one do this so personally and usually effectively as in medicine? I imagined myself, however, as a country doctor and did not dream that I would end up as a specialist in a metropolitan area! So I was launched easily onto this track and have always been grateful to my parents that they made it possible for me to go through medical school. It was their wise saving and foresight.

I started medical school in 1933, the same year that Hitler came to power in Germany. For the first year, in order to save money, I commuted to Vienna by train and street car, which took about 1 3/4 hours each way and this allowed a lot of time for studying on the train. The only unpleasant thing was getting up early in the morning to be on the train by 6 a.m. In the winter when one woke up to a freezing cold apartment, this was not too pleasant, but Papa often prepared hot chocolate for me the night before and kept it in a thermos for me for breakfast. I did enjoy the 8:00 a.m. anatomy lecture in the huge amphitheater of the Anatomical Institute on Waehringer-strasse. I never had much trouble with this subject since I was blessed with a very good visual memory and learned most of it by simply looking at pictures in the Atlas. Of course, we had also a great deal of dissecting to do, at least two hours daily. I still remember the feeling of disgust I had when we novices were standing in line to receive our first specimen for dissection. The rickety elevator came up from the basement and the orderly, a huge orangutan-faced man opened the door. He started distributing the pieces: a wrist with a hand, an elbow, a shoulder, an ankle – and so on, slopping the heavily carbolic acid smelling specimen into our hands with the smile of a sadist. It was the initiation rite, so to say, but only a few of us felt like throwing up. The moment we sat down at the dissecting table with our Atlas and started to identify the various structures, we began to feel happily intrigued with what we were doing.

In chemistry we also had lab besides the daily lecture, but biology (zoology) and physics were only lectures and rather boring with about 500-600 students trying to sit still and listen when we preferred to be out in the sun. I took the optional semester end exams (Colloquia) in the various subjects because this was an incentive to keep up with the material (there were no little weekly quizzes to help one, like here). This also entitled one to significantly reduced tuition fees for the next semester if one passed them satisfactorily. In this way I could afford to get a room in a student's dorm in Vienna for my second year, and stop commuting except on weekends. This made life much more pleasant. I could go now to the opera, the theater, concerts, and the museums in Vienna and soak up some of the culture for which we now travel thousands of miles and pay hundreds of dollars. I should have done it much more. We could go for a shilling (about 50 cents) to the Stehparterre (standing area) in the opera and for even less to the other theaters. I never saw any opera sitting down – until I came back after the war – and some of the Wagner operas are quite long. But we were young and enthusiastic enough to stand in line for an hour before the performance to get a better standing place. An unforgettable event was Furtwängler conducting Beethoven's Fifth and Sixth Symphony in the Konzerthaussaal. I had never heard such exciting music. In those days, people had no records and only rarely radios, so we had very little opportunity to hear good music except at live performances – and the good ones were only in Vienna.

During the summer vacation I always went on a week or ten days of "hut hopping" in the Alps, working my way further west every year. The anticipation and preparation for these trips was a great source of happiness during the whole year and helped me over many difficult moments when the going got rough and the work load too heavy. In July 1934, while I was climbing Grossglockner, our highest mountain, the news reached us of the assassination of our Chancellor Dollfuss by a Nazi gang. We were very upset, but the implications did not sink in, since we were political morons. Also the fact that there was more and more Nazi activity among the students did not open my eyes to what was coming. As a matter of fact, I did not even know that my best friend and colleague, Franz Bamer, had been a member of the illegal SS organization. There were many pessimists (like my Uncle Rudi) but I don't recall anyone who acted on their fears and actually left the country.

Most people, like myself, were just busy with their daily lives and would not even dream of giving up everything they had – their country, their position, their friends, for a threatening catastrophe, the severity of which was very difficult to imagine. Of course, we had heard much of what happened in Germany with the preparation for war. This had eliminated unemployment overnight and engendered enthusiasm with people flocking to the Nazi movement. The Nazis were encouraging the militaristic tendencies of the Germans and played on the resentment against the stupid and unjust Treaty of Versailles after the last war. We knew about the anti-Semitic Nuremberg laws that had progressively eliminated Jews from all walks of life in Germany. Many prominent ones had disappeared into concentration camps, many others had been forced to leave the country and the remaining ones were systematically robbed of everything they had, including frequently, their lives. Germany had only a very small minority of Jews (less that 1/2%). We in Austria had over 2%, so the self-deceptive argument was that even if Hitler took over Austria these inhuman Nuremberg race laws could never be enforced because there were too many Jews in our country. How differently it turned out! The laws were enforced even more ruthlessly!

The Tragedy of Hitler

On March 13, 1938, Hitler marched into Austria. In order to avoid unnecessary bloodshed, our chancellor Schuschnigg yielded to his ultimatum and ordered our troops not to resist. What then happened to our country has been written up in many books. I'll tell only our very personal story. The first tragedy that same day, believe it or not, was that our tame bird, a thistle finch that had been a pet for thirteen years, died. He had been an integral part of the family and my favorite – or I his. He would start singing the moment he heard my steps down in the entrance hall (we lived on the second floor.) and would come to sit on my shoulder or head when I entered the room. He used to come to our table at mealtime, drink from our glasses and bathed in them in bird fashion. Often, he shared our food. When the windows were closed, we usually left the door of his cage open so that he could go in or out as he pleased. He was so tame that I had an almost human contact with him and his death was a real blow and seemed, at the same time, a bad omen.

Our town was in an uproar. SA Troopers in their brown uniforms (where did they all come from overnight?), carrying swastika flags and wearing armbands, marched through the streets. In a way, this kind of circus was not too unfamiliar to us since other paramilitary organizations of the various Austrian political parties had such parades frequently in the past. Never had we seen so much enthusiastic response from the crowded sidewalks and windows. From our closed main street window, we could observe what was going on and we were frightened. How I hated their martial Nazi songs (Horst Wessel, etc.), their "Heil Hitler" and their anti-Semitic tirades.

I still remember the tears in Lislott's eyes when she came home from school in absolute dejection. She had not dared to join the parade like all her classmates, carrying the swastika flag. She felt – for the first time in her life – like an outcast. Kurt, who was working at the local courthouse as an apprentice judge, had been advised not to come back for the time being and to bring proof of being an Aryan in order to continue employment. This, according to Nuremberg laws, meant showing the baptismal certificates of all four grandparents. I was also soon informed by the university authorities to do the same in order to be allowed to continue my medical education. I was then in my last semester and I could not imagine that they could throw me out at this point. Nobody bothered us personally. On the contrary, all kinds of people whom we had only known superficially came to visit us and showed their concern with suggestions for help. We knew that it was dangerous to communicate with us and appreciated their friendship all the more.

Among these friends was also Peperl Schlamadinger, the son of our grocer who had his store on the street floor of our house at Bahngasse 2. He was studying economics in Vienna and was a very intelligent and bright young boy, very anti-Nazi. He was also, later on, one of the last people who still visited my father before his death when he was all alone in Vienna. Peperl himself was persecuted by the Nazis, but somehow managed to escape and to acquire, right after the war, a beautiful estate near Klagenfurt, an old castle which became both available and affordable due to the unusual circumstances. He remained a wonderful friend, and my brother Kurt or I visited him every time we went to Austria.

My classmate Wenger, a devout Catholic and now a Professor of Internal Medicine at the Rudolfspital in Vienna, was one of the few who knew about my racial background. He showed up one day in Wiener Neustadt and brought me news from the university. He had heard that the new authorities of the medical school had requested all non-Aryan students in their last semester (which was my case) to make an application to be allowed to continue and finish their medical education. It was hinted that 2% out of this group might be permitted to do so. I wrote up this application and went to Vienna to hand it in.

Before going to the university, I went to see my old friend and classmate, Franz Bamer, with whom I had been very close and who also knew that I was not "pure Aryan." Even though he had been a member of the previously illegal SS organization and now way up in their hierarchy, this had never bothered him. We had been friends for many years and he had always been a very decent fellow. I had written to him of the reason for my coming, namely asking for his help by intervening with the new potentates. When I called at his flat, his mother opened the door. She let me in and almost fell around my neck while tears rolled down her cheeks. She had always liked me and, I guess, was so upset about what had happened. I went into Franz's room and we discussed the situation. He was full of adventure stories of how he and his consorts had visited Jewish homes, and terrorized and plundered those "horrible people." As the Führer had said, there could be no pity for these "blood sucking monsters." I let him talk for awhile and then I said, "Do you know that I am Jewish, too, and do you really think that I am such a monster?" "But you have hardly any Jewish blood in you. That does not count." "No, I am 100% Jewish according to your friendly Nuremberg laws. He looked at me somewhat baffled and suspicious. "You don't mean it – it can't be!" "It is true," I said, and then there was a long silence. "Let's go to the Uni," he finally said. "I know the top man of the Nazi student organization very well. We have been buddies for many years and he'll do anything for me. I am sure I can explain your case to him and if he endorses your application, you will surely be allowed to finish the semester and get your diploma. After all, you are a decent fellow and only a few months from getting your degree and you should not he affected by all this."

So we took the streetcar together to the university and I waited outside while he went up to plead my case. I had no hopes that he would get anywhere, but thought it was very nice and brave of him to try. It. took a long time before he finally showed up, his face drawn with hidden rage and disappointment. He had had to wait a long time before he was admitted to see the big boss and when he presented my story, he was reprimanded in a very rude manner for daring to intervene for a Jew. His loyalty to the Führer was questioned, etc., etc. It was a rough awakening for him! I put in my application through official channels anyway and then went back to Wiener Neustadt to await the course of events.

It took a few weeks for us to really grasp what had happened and to accept the fact that we had been deprived of the right to live an ordinary, decent life; that we had lost our country and we would have to leave in order to survive. No one put this more succinctly than good old *Kurt Nistler*, who became for me, and many others, a shining beacon of humanity in those trying times.

I had not known him before. Onkel Rudi introduced us. He lived with his charming, petite wife, Lilly, in a tiny inconspicuous flat not far from the opera in one of those very ancient houses of the Inner City (Annagasse). The most impressive thing in their main room was a huge library which showed a heavy accent on old Greek and Medieval literature, much on philosophy, history and art. He had, in the past, made two attempts to get a university education, first in law and then in medicine, but each time he could not finish because he ran out of money and had to take a job to support himself. He spoke five languages fluently, and frequently quoted in Latin or Greek. He had a very quick mind and a good heart. For the last ten years, he had been working as a sleeping car conductor and had traveled all across Europe from Ostende to Athens or Istanbul. He did not dislike his job because he enjoyed using his languages in meeting people of different nationalities The job also allowed him a lot of time for reading on the trains.

When the Hitler mess started, he found a new challenge, which he took up with tremendous devotion and cunning – helping Jewish and politically endangered friends to escape. It was a nerve-wracking endeavor, but he saved I don't know how many lives and helped many others to get some of their possessions across the borders so that they didn't have to start a new existence in a foreign country, penniless. He paid a heavy price for all this – two years in a concentration camp in Dachau and a premature death from a heart attack soon after the end of the war. Of all the people I knew, he had the most foresight and it was this foresight that saved our lives.

There were many others besides Nistler who, in their consternation and disgust with what was going on, showed their concern and helped in whatever way they could, most importantly by moral support. I had not realized that we had so many friends because we never had an active social life at all. It was these demonstrations of friendship, which we knew always meant danger for our friends, that made this period tolerable and strengthened our belief in the good side of human nature at a moment when so much meanness was surfacing. It was hard not to lose faith in humanity with all the killing, tortures in concentration camps, officially condoned robbery, expulsion from jobs and unending humiliation of perfectly innocent people that kept happening all around us. In retrospect, it was probably this show of friendship and decency that made it possible for me to survive all the misery without permanent resentment. I also learned the lesson that one must never judge people by groups, but only as single individuals, and even then to try to distinguish between the good and the bad in each person – if one must judge at all.

Since Papa had been in retirement already for three years, he was not immediately exposed to any humiliation except for having to wear the yellow armband when this became mandatory after 1939. As a former state employee, he continued to receive his pension until he died in Vienna in December, 1941. Somehow he seemed too old to grasp what was really going on and was unable to do anything constructive. Uncle Rudi immediately applied for a visa to the United States and advised Kurt to do the same. The affidavit for both of them was given by Uncle Robert, Uncle Rudi's brother in Ohio. Uncle Paul, who lived with his parents in Vienna at the time, became the key figure in our whole emigration story.

An old friend of Paul's called him on April 1st to tell him that while sitting in a coffee house browsing through a Jewish newspaper, he had seen an ad from Japan for a forging engineer. Paul thought at first it was an April Fool's joke, but it wasn't. Telegrams went back and forth to Japan (Who had ever heard of that country except through "Madame Butterfly"?), and by the middle of April Paul had received a contract as an engineer for three years with a good salary and paid transportation. It sounded like a miracle. As we found out later, the ad had been inserted at the instigation of a German Jewish engineer, Mr. Rosenberg, who was living in Japan and had connections to a Japanese factory that needed a forging engineer. He realized what was going on in Europe and saw an opportunity to help. Paul dug up his old engineering books and drawings to brush up day and night on a subject he had worked on fifteen to eighteen years ago, and by the beginning of May he was ready to leave (via Lloyd Triestino from Italy). He was the first one of us to leave and I still remember that we all went to the train station in Wiener Neustadt when he passed through, to say good bye. In the few minutes that the train was stopped, he had a very important message for us. The day before, he had hit the jackpot in the State lottery! There was no time, of course, for him to receive the money and as a Jew, he probably would never have gotten it anyway. But somehow he managed to turn the whole thing over to Carl, who as an "Aryan" could collect and keep the very substantial sum for us and the grandparents. This literally saved all our lives, because without it, we would never have been able to afford the transportation cost and other expenses to get us out.

Toward the end of April, I was notified that I would be allowed to finish my medical education in Vienna "until further notice." I had hoped for this, but still had prepared myself for rejection. Why was I chosen as being among the 2%? Because I was Catholic? I'll never know. I went back to the university, studying like a fool to be ready for the final exams that started with Pathology and Pharmacology at the end of June.

I spent quite a lot of time with Bamer. He was always an excellent student and could explain things in such clear and unforgettable ways that I learned a lot from him. By that time, he also had fallen in love with a half-Jewish girl, a classmate of ours, and this further changed his political outlook. Being always very outspoken, he had got into a lot of trouble over this matter, and if he had not been an illegal party member for so long before the Anschluss, he would have been in a concentration camp by then.

My heavy work schedule kept me so busy that I had little mind or ear for what was going on around me (as usual). Uncle Rudi and Aunt Hedi left at the end of May for Switzerland because he felt it was too dangerous to wait for his U S quota in Vienna. I recall the last time I saw him. He was terribly pessimistic for the future, hated the idea of going to America and was actually already then a broken man. As we walked through the streets in Vienna near his flat, we met an older man who looked obviously Jewish and, like us, did not wear the ubiquitous swastika pin. The two of them talked a little, exchanging some dismal news (there was lots around) and then we parted. "Do you know who that was?" Uncle Rudi asked me. "No, how should I?" "That was Poldi Huber." Poldi Huber was a character known to everyone in Vienna, like Charlie Brown or Dennis the Menace here. He portrayed a young Viennese boy from one of the outlying districts where people speak a very funny and coarse dialect. The stories about him, written in the first person, were hilarious, both in content and language, and many of his sayings had become famous quotes in everyday language. We had spent many happy hours of laughter over these books, and I could not believe that this old haggard and miserable man that we had just met had been the author of those delightfully comical stories. When Uncle Rudi left, Nistler was with them and they got all their most important belongings across the border.

Papa's family did not fare well. Uncle Victor, the socialist congressman (Papa's brother-in-law) was imprisoned right away on two accounts – being socialist and Jewish. He never came out alive. His wife, Aunt Rosa, managed to get out to Sweden through some Swedish socialist friends of theirs. But her son, Egon, was sent to Dachau and his wife and baby daughter fled to her parents in Bern, Switzerland. Egon, miraculously, survived Dachau and somehow managed to get out to England just before the war started in 1939. He never saw his wife again. Papa's other sister, Anna, and her husband who had owned a bookstore, were older people and had at first only their store taken away. They later perished in a concentration camp in Poland. I saw them last just before leaving Austria, when I stayed with them overnight in Vienna. They were lovely people and I felt awful when I had to say good bye to them. I had liked them so much because Aunt Anna had always been full of jokes and her husband had been my companion on my first hiking trip in the Hohen Tauern.

I passed my exams without much trouble and immediately started preparing for the remaining ones in the fall. However, in July, Kurt and I decided to go for the last time on a hiking trip to the mountains near Bad Gastein, in the Ankogl and Hochalmspitz area. In order to stay at the various huts, one had to show one's membership card in the Alpine Club. We had our old cards, but according to the new race law, our membership had been automatically revoked. We felt a little embarrassed in showing our cards, but nothing happened. Unfortunately, the weather was not too good so we cut the trip short and went to Salzburg instead. Kurt had fallen in love with that town the year before, and I had never seen it. I could understand now why he liked the place so much and my emotionally motivated attempt to go back there to practice, in 1970, stemmed from my impressions during this first visit. That was the last we enjoyed of Austria.

Through the help of Nistler, who had a friend at the Yugoslav consulate, both Kurt and I got a visiting visa for Yugoslavia. At the beginning of September, Kurt left with

38

Nistler for Zagreb to wait for his U S visa and quota in a safer place. There were good letters from Paul, who was working hard to prepare entrance papers for Japan for his parents and all of us. He seemed to like his job and the courteous way the Japanese treated him. To us, this all sounded so unreal and exotic, but it was good news – much needed good news. At the end of September, I could continue taking my final exams again. It was like steeplechasing, and I passed one about every week: Internal Medicine, Pediatrics, Psychiatry, Neurology, Surgery and OB-GYN. So things went well on that front, but then my parents in Wiener Neustadt were "politely" notified that we had better move to Vienna since no Jews were allowed to live in the provinces anymore. That was a major hassle, because it was very difficult to find a flat with the law of the land for racial discrimination. Lislott, who had grown up fast in this last half year (she had her seventeenth birthday one day after Hitler marched into Austria), became a very efficient and fearless helper in these family matters now that Kurt was gone.

In reminiscing about these times, I don't quite understand why I didn't become rebellious at all these degrading and more or less subtle persecutions that were meted out to us every day. Was it my docile nature or the fact that it seemed completely hopeless and insane to rebel? Having lived under a totalitarian terror regime, I can understand Solzhenitsyn's stories and can see them as true. My reaction was always one of escape, not of standing up against overwhelming odds. I can see that if one grows up in this country, the USA, with its deeply ingrained tradition of "inalienable human rights," it is very hard to understand what it means to live in a totalitarian atmosphere and may, therefore, minimize its dangers. On the other hand, this tradition may make it possible to react against any oppression before freedoms are lost.

Soon after Kurt left, all "non-Aryans" who had been issued passports were asked to return them to have a huge red "J" stamped onto the front page. It had become increasingly difficult for any of us to obtain entrance, or even transit visas from any country without this "J." This "friendly gesture" surely did not help. America was practically the only country that did not change its immigration policies in our disfavor. But the quota system and the need for an affidavit made this a lengthy procedure, particularly for us from Austria, whose quota had been exhausted a few weeks after Hitler took over. All countries refused to take us in, either because they were afraid of penniless refugees or because they were afraid of Hitler and did not wish to offend him by being nice to us. There were some exceptions however – like Holland, Denmark and Sweden, but you had to have very good connections. The only place that really did not care was China, which was so far away and so involved in its struggle with Japan that this problem was too infinitesimal to be noticed at all. So, many of those Jews who had not been prepared for the debacle, fled to the Far East and formed the Ghetto in Shanghai. China could not care less about a red "J," thank God!

Then came the big pogrom of November 9th, the "Kristallnacht." Hitler unleashed all the cruelty of his hordes on the Jews allegedly in retaliation of an attack on the German Ambassador in Paris by an angry Jew. This time the vox populi was not to speak primarily against the wealthy and prominent Jews – they had mostly left the country by then or their belongings had been confiscated already – but against all Jews, including the old, the sick and the poor. They were dragged from their homes to some detention center for interrogation with or without beatings. In the Jewish sector of Vienna, where there still were a few Jewish owned stores, the windows were smashed and the furniture broken to pieces and the owners taken away. Some never returned – many were released after a few days because there simply was no place to put all these people.

When all this broke loose, I was staying with my grandparents in Vienna because I was studying for the exams. That very morning I was at the very peaceful Dermatological Clinic in the Allgemeine Krankenhaus taking a preparatory course. When I walked home in the afternoon, the streets were deserted except for some gangs of brownshirted brutes out for more loot and torture. I was glad I had iron rimmed heels that made a loud clapping sound on the granite pavement when I walked briskly. This gave me a certain sense of security as I passed some of these gangs, seemingly unconcerned. For awhile, I thought one of these guys was following me, but I kept up my regular pace, without turning around and whistled some melody (to myself?) and nothing happened! But when I came home, the door of our flat was locked and nobody answered the bell. I didn't know what to do. Where were my grandparents? I knocked at the neighbor's door, but got no response there either. They were friends of my grandparents and also Jewish. Finally I found somebody in the building and was told that the brownshirts had been there and had taken a few people along – nobody knew where.

I went down a few blocks to Uncle George's flat (Anita's father). They were the only relatives we had left in Vienna. He was a retired Supreme Court Judge, a delightful and very respected old gentleman whom we all revered and loved. They had been Catholic since childhood and in his youth, in the time of the Austrian monarchy, he had been a private tutor of the Crown Prince. They had not been molested previously because of their exceptional position, but when I arrived there, three young high school punks in brown shirts and swastika armbands were talking to the old gentleman in the most insulting and threatening way. It was a very ugly scene and I would have loved to kick those bullies in the ass – but I knew better. They finally left without arresting him. Apparently they had not intended more than to show their power and to insult him. Both he and Aunt Marie (Mama's cousin and Uncle Rudi's sister) were thoroughly shaken but were glad to see me. They thought it was a miracle that nothing had happened to me since all the younger Jewish people had been taken to prison. They had no idea where my grandparents were. I stayed with them overnight, worrying about what had happened to them and also to my parents in Wiener Neustadt. Next day things seemed to calm down; but I did not leave the house until noon, when there were again more people in the streets, just to run over to my grandparents' flat. What a relief to find them back in not too bad shape. They had spent only the one night at some police station, together with many others, and had survived it quite well. Their flat was a mess, because the visitors had gone through all the drawers and thrown everything all over the floor. I helped them clean up and then rushed to the train to Wiener Neustadt to see what had happened there. We had been lucky again – nobody had touched my parents. Had we been forgotten, or spared? I would like to assume the latter.

Even before this horrible episode, our plans for the future – as far as I could make them – had been set. Now they jelled overnight. It was clear that I would not be permitted to take my final four exams (Dermatology, Ophthalmology, Hygiene and Forensic Medicine) and therefore would not get my degree. There was no reason to stay in Austria a day longer.

We had written to Paul to try to obtain some entrance permit for Japan so that Kurt and I could travel together to the Far East. Kurt's American quota seemed in the nebulous future and Yugoslavia not too safe a place either, so he felt he might as well wait for it in Japan. He had made several good friends through introduction by Nistler, and supported himself by giving English lessons to Jewish families. He lived in a hole-in-the-wall off the kitchen of a young Yugoslav widow. She and her pretty teenaged daughter were very nice to him and, if I remember well, he corresponded with them for a long time and even saw them on one of his recent visits there. The tiny room was so small that there was just enough area for the bed, but to get into it one had to climb over the posts at the foot end. At least it had a window near the head end. We both had tickets for the Conte Rosso of the Lloyd Triestino Orient Line and he was just waiting for its departure on January 4, 1939.

I still helped to find a flat for my parents and Lislott in Vienna and got my things ready to leave. The problem was that my passport with the Yugoslav visa had, in the meantime, been stamped with the red "J" so there was a good possibility that I would be refused entry at the Yugoslav border. Nistler was the first one aware of this since he traveled this route frequently. If they would turn me back, the Nazi border guards would have sent me straight to a German concentration camp. So what was to be done? We went together to his friend at the Yugoslav embassy for advice, and this man came up with a brilliant idea: take the plane straight to Belgrade, which is in the middle of the country, and pass the controls there. With my ticket for the Conte Rosso leaving a few weeks later, there was a chance that they might not send me all the way back to the Austrian border, but let me stay a little while in the country (after all I had a visa) until I could move on. Naturally, I was willing to take this lesser chance. After the conference at the embassy, Nistler and I drove off in a taxi, and when I dropped him off at his house we said good bye in the car. He kissed me and said, "May God keep you." Then he handed me a beautiful black wallet as a farewell gift – which I still have as a souvenir of an unforgettable moment and a dear friend.

I had to get all my papers that were required of Jews who wanted to leave the country – proof that I did not owe any taxes, that there were no legal proceedings pending against me, that I was exempt from military service (which half -Jews could not get), etc., etc. I still remember going for the latter to the Army Headquarters in Wiener Neustadt. Papa accompanied me. He did not say much, but I could feel how he suffered from all this. We were leaving, one after the other, and there was no way he could be of help. Practically all we could take along was a suitcase and what we had in our head. At least he had made it possible for us to have an education. I talked about the uncertainty of the future and that, of course, he and Mama would soon follow us wherever we would be, but he was not very committal on this point. He felt that he had his pension and therefore financial security in Austria, while we probably had a hard time ahead of us and would not be able to support him. Paul had offered to bring *all* of us out to Japan, but Papa did not want to accept his invitation. He had his pride and prejudice and simply did not see the situation realistically. He still took me to the train station on December 3rd when I left for the Vienna airport and we said good bye, waving our handkerchiefs until we were out of sight. It was the last time I saw him. I blamed myself afterwards that I had not been able to convince him to leave with Mama and my grandparents for Japan. I was not forceful enough, because somehow I could see his point of view and, moreover, he promised to follow us boys as soon as we were in a secure enough position to ask him to come and join us. As the drama unfolded, he did stay behind alone when Mama left with her parents for the Far East in February, 1939. Lislott left soon after that, on a Quaker children's transport to England.

Hilda and Jacob Bock at their wedding in 1909

Uncle Paul, circa 1940

Brother Kurt Bock, 1934

Graduation 1941

Dr. Snapper with his interns at graduation. Rudi Bock on the right

Student outing in Peking's Western Hills, 1940

Trude and Pater Maas at the Buddhist Temple, circa 1945

48

Pierre Teilhard de Chardin

Dr. Adolf Franceschetti

Simple Pleasures
Photograph by Hedda Hammer

Emigration to China

I left Vienna on December 4th, 1938. I had never been on an airplane before in my life and was so excited that I could not think much of all the pain of leaving so many beloved people behind under those dismal circumstances. I also was very apprehensive about what might happen in Belgrade on arrival with my "J" on the passport. It was a gray and misty day and as we flew over the Austrian border, a sudden feeling of relief came over me, but I quickly caught myself realizing that I was far from safe and still very much within the reach of this murderous regime. We flew rather low over the Hungarian plains, stopped briefly in Budapest and then flew on to Belgrade. The one comforting thought was that I knew Kurt would be picking me up at the airport. As we stepped out of the plane I prayed that this would be the last time I saw the detested swastika insignia. And then came the passport and customs check. I saw Kurt standing at the far side of the exit bars and we exchanged smiles of happiness. The officer looked at my passport and immediately looked startled by the red "J." He leafed through it, found the Yugoslav visa and showed even more consternation. Obviously he did not know what to make of it and so he asked me to step aside while he passed the other passengers through. Most of them were obviously Fifth Column German "tourists." Then he called his boss and they talked for awhile with serious faces "You entered the country illegally and are under arrest," was what they eventually came up with. In the meantime, Kurt had worked his way up towards me and tried to talk to the officers. "Who are you?" they asked him. "His brother." "Show me your passport!" Hesitantly, Kurt pulled out his passport. What could he do! "How come you smuggled yourself into this country without a "J," you dirty Jew?" Kurt tried to explain that he had entered Yugoslavia perfectly legally with a valid visa before the Nazis stamped the "J" into his passport. "You are under arrest, too," was the final answer.

Fortunately, Kurt had been recommended by his friends in Zagreb to a well-known local attorney and had discussed the matter with him before coming to the airport. Now he somehow managed to get the chief officer to speak to the attorney on the phone. After this conversation, we both were allowed to go free, but they kept our passports. What next! We went to see the attorney, whose wife happened to be sick in bed with a bad thrombophlebitis of the leg. He was very eager for me – coming from the famous medical school in Vienna – to examine her, which I did gladly. I suggested that he try to get some Prontosil (the first sulfa drug that had just come on the market in Germany) in addition to the conservative treatment that she had been getting. I did not hear whether it helped her, but I know that it helped us, because he went to the chief of police with a substantial amount of money that Kurt had borrowed from friends in Zagreb and came back with both of our passports. So we were finally free – and happy – and took the next train to Zagreb.

Zagreb was a revelation to me. I had never felt myself a Jew and plainly refused to have my identity changed from one day to the next by some crazy laws. We had always moved in Christian circles and had had very little contact with orthodox Jews – certainly not enough to understand, except very superficially, what it was to be a Jew. The last ten months had changed all that. Even though we had been lucky enough to escape unhurt, we had come to feel very personally what it meant to be a victim of virulent and ugly anti-Semitism. Now in Zagreb, and later in Shanghai, we experienced how the Jews (probably down through the ages) had coped with this problem of recurrent persecution. Converted or not, we were taken in by the Jewish community like one of them!

I was placed with the lovely Haas family, whose hospitality was unbelievable, so that I felt at home immediately. They were older people and had a son of Kurt's age who had also applied for immigration to the United States. In Yugoslavia, people used to eat very well and Mrs. Haas was an excellent cook. Since it was Chanukka season, we enjoyed her excellent cuisine. What meant more to us was the general concern and kindness they showed. I remember one instance in particular. With Nistler's help, Kurt had smuggled a few old ducats (gold coins from the time of the Austrian monarchy) that Papa had collected and kept for emergencies as well as some English pounds in banknotes. We knew that on leaving Yugoslavia we would be thoroughly searched at the border and that there would be no Nistler around this time. So what to do? We had discussed the problem with the Haas family and one morning Mrs. Haas came beaming to the breakfast table. "I've got the answer for you! I'll make you a coin purse with a double inside layer and you can put your coins between these two layers before I lace up the borders." She was an expert leather worker and had found this solution in a dream! The purse kept its secret for over twenty-five years until it was opened by one of my overcurious children. I should never have given its secret away.

The husband of one of Kurt's English pupils (Milrad) who had a small cosmetics factory, came up with a solution to smuggle the banknotes. He wrapped them in tin foil and put them inside a large tube of toothpaste. There were many other people who were very helpful and nice, among them the Catholic bishop of Zagreb. He was very concerned about the refugee problem and particularly wanted to help the Catholics among them, people like us. Kurt kept in touch with him through all these years and when he went to Rome a few years ago, he made an appointment (long ahead of time) to see him. By then the bishop had become a cardinal.

I remember one episode in Zagreb that still makes me feel uneasy when I think of it. Someone had recommended a man to us who was supposed to be able to remove the red "J" from my passport for a fee. After the experience at the Belgrade airport, it was probably an understandable idea, but I was very dubious about such falsifications. Kurt and I met the man in some side alley and he looked at my passport for a long time, holding it against the light and feeling the red ink and finally said he could do it. Kurt looked at me and said, "What do you think? It is your passport and your decision." I looked at the man's face and did not like it at all, "I think I had better accept fate and run the risks of the 'J,'" I said finally, and we parted.

A few days before leaving for Triest, I got a letter from Paul with a long enclosure written in Japanese. It was a fake contract for me as a plant physician at the factory where Paul was working and had been made out so that the Japanese immigration authorities would let me land with my "J." It had arrived in the nick of time – what luck!

It was hard to leave the many nice people we had met in Zagreb with the great uncertainty of what was going to happen to all of us. Would we see each other again? We left Zagreb early on January 3rd and had no problem getting through the strict border controls into Italy, where we boarded the Conte Rosso in Triest the same evening. I had never seen a large ocean liner before, had never seen the sea – and everything was very exciting. We had passage in the crowded tourist class and soon found out that almost all our fellow passengers were

German or Austrian refugees – literally "all in the same boat" – destination Shanghai, the only escape hatch!

During the first night, we crossed the Adriatic to Venice, where we could go sightseeing for a few hours. I enjoyed the architecture around St. Mark's Square and a short ride on a gondola along the canals before we finally settled back in on the ship for the long voyage. The next morning, we had a rather rough sea and it was very cold and windy as we sailed south of Crete and saw the high snow covered peaks of that island as we passed by. I had not realized that Crete had such high mountains. Then came Port Said and the first taste of the Orient with hordes of peddlers offering their tourist junk, shouting up to us from their little boats floating alongside the ship. It got much warmer as we passed through the Suez Canal and became really hot in the Red Sea. We had started in fur coats in Venice and now could hardly tolerate a shirt. The desert on either side of the Canal was spooky, and I could not believe how people could live in the tiny shacks that we saw from the ship. We even passed some camel caravans. The light was extremely bright and hurt our unaccustomed eyes. Since we were on an Italian liner, we stopped in Massawa next, the supply port for the Italian expeditionary forces in Ethiopia. Italy, coming at the tail end of the colonial period, had conquered that country only a few years previously. All I can remember of the dismally desolate area is the phosphorescence of the wave crests as we approached the harbor in the evening. It was an eerie sight, as if the sea were on fire. I was glad to learn that it was only due to tiny luminous plankton and not from a burning oil spill.

What a relief to finally got out into the open Indian Ocean where the heat was much less oppressive. I tried to study English, reading *Reader's Digest* with Kurt's and the dictionary's help.

My four years of English in High School was a good basis, but being able to read Shakespeare didn't mean at all that one was able to speak or understand the language. In most other ways, I was equally poorly prepared for the tremendous changes in our lives. We had been so busy just surviving these last ten months and I had been so involved with trying to finish my exams that there was no time to even imagine what our future contact with the Far East would entail. I knew practically nothing about Japan and China or, for that matter, about India, where we were to land next. After the glimpse I got from the ship in the two Oriental ports we had touched, I realized how provincial and narrow our education had been, because our horizon barely reached beyond the Austrian border and my summer in France had extended it only very little compared to what we were getting into now. We met a very nice young Indian teacher on the ship who was on his way home and spent hours listening to his stories. Even through the eyes of a westernized Indian, his country seemed fantastic – its enormous size, its many different religions and races, their struggle for independence under Ghandi, their overpopulation, poverty and disease. There were more people living in India than in the whole of Europe and I had not even been consciously aware of their existence.

We had, for the first time, several days of uninterrupted open ocean voyage. The weather was good and the sea calm. I used to spend hours at the bow of the ship, looking over the waves, watching for schools of flying fish or porpoises that accompanied us, or often just staring straight ahead at the wide horizon, wondering what the future had in store for us. In Bombay, we saw only the waterfront because we were not allowed to go on land with our passports. But in Ceylon, they had apparently not yet been gripped by fear of an invasion by Jewish refugees, so we were allowed to go ashore. We saw the botanical gardens with their fascinating exotic flowers – a whole new world! We followed the crowd to a Catholic mission where some of our compatriots begged embarrassingly for money from the priest. It was hot and humid, but not as bad as Bombay. I don't remember having seen too much evidence of the poverty and hunger that I encountered on later visits to India, probably because we did not drive anywhere near the poor districts. We were happy to be back on the ship again, though, after this little outing and were glad to hear the familiar gong that regularly called us to meals.

In Bombay, a number of Chinese passengers had joined us and among them was a quiet, very distinguished looking elderly gentleman who used to sit out on deck most of the time reading. We had heard that these people had attended an international YMCA conference in Bombay. One day Kurt started a conversation with Mr. Ch'uan, the man who had attracted our special attention. He was aware of what went on in Europe and why there were so many unusual passengers on the ship. He listened patiently to our story. The next day, when Kurt introduced me to him, Mr. Chu'an hinted that he might be able to help me. As it turned out, he was a Shanghai banker who had spent many years in the United States and was a trustee of the Peiping Union Medical College (PUMC). He promised to introduce me to Dr. Houghton, the director of the PUMC, on our arrival in Shanghai. I had never heard of the PUMC and was surprised to hear that there was an American Medical School in Peking, an institution built and run by the Rockefeller Foundation since 1922. I had planned to apply to the medical schools of Hong Kong and Manila if I should not be able to get admitted in Japan to finish my medical education. It seemed like a fantastic stroke of luck if this acquaintance with Mr. Ch'uan would open an opportunity for me to get my degree.

In both Singapore and Hong Kong we were allowed to go ashore. I was struck by the fancy and often palatial homes in the residential district, in contrast to the dwellings of the poor people. Here I also saw my first rickshaws. What a degradation of a human being to be a work horse! But the people – white, brown and yellow – who sat in them didn't seem in the least disturbed. They were used to it. At that time, I could not imagine ever using this mode of transportation myself - but I did, of course, later in Peking. We liked Hong Kong very much despite the heat and humidity. It is a fascinating city, beautifully located and we enjoyed the view from the top of the cable car on Victoria Island. The downtown area was bustling with active people and made a fairly prosperous impression, judging from the stores and the big hotels and banking buildings. A large number of people lived in their boats, forming whole colonies on the shores, because they were too poor to find housing ashore, which was very limited in any case. If someone had told me that there would be three times as many people living on this small spot of land a decade later, I would not have believed it possible. But that is what happened when millions of Chinese refugees streamed into Hong Kong with the Communist takeover of mainland China. The population rose from a little over a million to four million!

Then came Shanghai. We had not the slightest idea what would happen. We only knew that we had our tickets to leave three weeks later on a British liner for Japan. This was a very reassuring fact and we felt much luckier than all our other fellow refugees. To our great surprise, everything had been organized by the Shanghai Jewish community. They had the full list of our names, picked us up from the pier and brought us to the local synagogue where we were fed and given blankets to sleep on the floor. We could not believe it! Kurt made friends with a pleasant looking girl who was in charge of the kitchen, Aziza Abraham. She was the daughter of one of the active and wealthy members of the community, with whom we kept up a correspondence for many years thereafter. They were Arabian Jews who had lived in Shanghai for generations; we were invited to their big house several times during our stay in Shanghai. It was amazing how this whole "rescue operation" had been organized and how well it functioned because it was no small task to feed and put up these masses of people (I guess we had about 500 on our ship) that came in every two weeks or so. After a few days we rented a small room in the French concession to have more privacy and a bed instead of the hard but hospitable floor of the synagogue – and also to make room for new arrivals.

We had made an appointment with Mr. Ch'uan to meet Dr. Houghton, who happened to be on business in Shanghai and was staying in one of the big hotels on the Bund. Kurt went with me because I still had a lot of trouble understanding English and this was too important a meeting to foul up because of a language barrier. Dr. Houghton was very friendly, but not outright optimistic because he was not the one to make the decision. However, I had the feeling he wanted to help. He suggested I send an application for admission to the college which he would endorse for consideration by the appropriate committee. So Kurt wrote a long letter, explaining all the circumstances, and after Dr. Houghton added his remarks, it was sent off to Peking. I really felt like I was living under a lucky star! Most of the refugees stayed in Shanghai and had a very hard time eking out a meager existence in a totally alien culture, depending mostly on relief or the good will of the foreign and Jewish community. It was a miserable life for most of them. I was glad to leave Shanghai. It was a depressing, strange and mysterious place, and I felt sorry for many of the people who had come with us on the Conte Rosso and whom we had come to know a little.

We sailed for Japan on an almost empty P & O liner. The stewards had plenty of time and one of them, obviously an Irishman, liked to tell us long stories about the hostility of the Irish for the British which we, of course, didn't know anything about. They don't seem to have made much progress in the last thirty-five years! Another thing that was new to me, at least, was that the English served jam and other sweets with their meat dishes and that their food in general was not too tasty. Otherwise, those three days passed rapidly in anticipation of arriving at our destination and seeing Paul again. We did not want the same thing to happen to us on entering Japan that made it so miserable in Belgrade. I had my letter from Paul's factory and was to land in Yokohama with my "J" passport. Kurt had to avoid being incriminated again because of me, so he decided to get off in Kobe, where our ship first landed, pass through the controls alone and take the train to Tokyo (Kawasaki) where Paul lived. It worked. He was admitted with all the courtesy and friendliness typical of the Japanese, because of his German passport. What a farce it all was!

I had another day's voyage along the beautiful coast and, as we approached our destination, Mt. Fujiyama was an impressive landmark. Engineer Rosenberg, Paul and Kurt met me at the pier in Yokohama and it was really great to see them. I had no trouble at all passing the immigration officer. They studied my letter and did not even give me a suspicious look. It took me a little while to stop staring at the strange features and dress of the people, their way of walking and talking and other mannerisms that are so striking when one sees the Japanese at first. Paul's little Japanese "birdhouse" in Kawasaki was very cute and right across the street from the Rosenbergs. He had an amah who cooked and cleaned for him and was also very nice to us. We very quickly caught on to the Japanese way of taking off our shoes before entering the house as well as sleeping on the soft floor (tatami) on the bed rolls that were kept in the closets during the day. The Japanese way of taking a bath in the small wooden tubs with the built-in heater is really a great invention – ecology long before the word was invented! We felt at home right away and happy to be able to relax a little after all the tension in Europe and the traveling. I still remember how I enjoyed hearing some of the familiar records that Paul had brought along from Austria, like Beethoven's Trio Serenade and a Chopin Prelude. Whenever I hear those now, 1 see myself in his Japanese house and remember the pleasant feeling of having arrived in a safe haven after a storm at sea.

Engineer Rosenberg was a very interesting man with a profound knowledge of Japan, having lived there most of his adult life. He was also a good hiker, in the good old European tradition, and took me once on a long trip down the Isu Peninsula. We always stayed at those neat hotels with hot springs, so I got exposed to the great Japanese hobby of enjoying hot baths. Men and women bathe together naked in those large indoor pools that one can only enter after one has cleaned oneself extensively in the various antechambers. It takes a long time to dip into these very hot pools, unless one is a Japanese and used to the scorching heat of the water. One gets cooked like a crab. The other hotel guests stared at us like monsters from another planet with our hairy, white skins and our long straight legs. I was not sure how much they appreciated sharing their pools with us. What I liked best in these places and anywhere in the Japanese houses was the marvelously exact woodwork which makes all the windows and doors so attractive. The architecture of their temples, all in wood in pagoda style, and their gardens is really very artistic and beautiful. Here was another culture, completely different from ours, that I had had no idea of. This was a large world, fascinating and beautiful, even if it was infested with quite a few madmen, too.

Peking (Beijing)

To my great surprise, a reply from the PUMC arrived in less than two weeks after our arrival in Japan, but unfortunately it was negative. I still have that letter (see appendix) and also the one that Kurt composed in answer to it. I kept them as "historic documents" in my life's history. Their main argument against accepting me was that I could not speak Chinese. There was no way to deny that. I didn't even know enough English, so sadly, I accepted their decision. Not so Kurt! He immediately sat down and composed a reply, painting a dismal picture of my predicament – the interruption of my medical education so close before the end, having to leave my home country, etc., etc., and promising that I would study Chinese or whatever they required if they would give me a chance. I thought he was a bit pushy and maybe promised too much, but the letter went off and to our great surprise and joy, in another two weeks we received a positive answer. This change in their attitude was owing to one man, as I heard later. He was Peter Kronfeld, the Professor of Ophthalmology, a former Austrian who had emigrated to the States after his residency in Vienna under Fuchs and was a professor in Chicago, now on a four year assignment in Peking. He was a member of the admission committee, but had been absent from the first meeting when they had decided against my admission to the school. This time he was consulted, and understanding the situation, he had swung the scale in my favor. I'll never forget what he did for me by this decision.

My admission to the PUMC was subject to several rather demanding conditions, but I didn't bother to worry about them. I accepted, of course, since this was my only chance. I had heard in the meantime from Hong Kong and Manila, where I had also applied, and from the Japanese medical school that I had approached and they all would not have taken me. The PUMC admission committee accepted my five years of medical education, in Vienna (actually, I was only three weeks away from getting my diploma) in lieu of their entrance examination. Then I would have to pass all the examinations of their first three years before I would be enter the fourth year classes in September. They also required an examination in spoken Chinese by that time and insisted that I should stay at the student's dorm (Wenham Hall). The last one was the easiest demand by far. I had a great time there.

So I left for Peking by train as soon as I could get everything ready. Mama and my grandparents were to arrive (without Papa) in Japan about two weeks after I left, but with such a heavy work schedule ahead of me for the next six months, I didn't feel I should stay for their arrival. Paul gave me the money (all in all about $350) to get me through the first year and a half, including the minimal tuition. During the following intern years, I could be on my own already. It was a long but interesting trip. The Japanese countryside is beautiful and the trains were good and clean, the food very tasteless. People were polite, but suspicious, and there were many uniformed people around – after all the country was at war with China and had a huge occupation army on the mainland. We crossed over to Korea during the night, arriving at sunrise in Fusan.

I had noticed a nice looking man on the train after Kobe, who shared the same compartment with me. Again on the ferry, he was in the same berth with me and then I recognized him again, this time in uniform, as we passed through customs in Fusan. He gave me a broad smile and I realized that he had been spying on me. Fortunately, I had not told him anything important in the little conversation he had tried to make. Also, in Korea and all through Manchuria, I had the feeling of being watched all the time, since the same faces kept showing up.

In Manchuria, the train grew very crowded and dirty, and the people were poorly dressed and their features changed. We kept going and going, day and night. There was still a lot of snow on the vast plains and the heating in the cars was mostly animal (or human) heat. Finally, I arrived in Peking. The train station is right next to the main South Gate (Ch'ien Men), a towering building accentuating the very high city hall – an impressive sight. Hundreds of people milling around, shouting and gesticulating in a strange sing-song tongue, and offering their services as porter. I had been instructed to take a rickshaw and go to Wenham Hall, the PUMC dorm, so I said to one of those hustling Chinese, "Wenham Hall," and to my great surprise, he seemed to understand, smiled, took my suitcase and led me out to his rickshaw. There I was, sitting in one of those vehicles that I had so disapproved of when I first saw them in Singapore, yet it seemed rather natural. The galloping "horseman" in front of me didn't seem to mind it at all – he joked with the other coolies as we rode along and seemed to have a good time – obviously expecting an extra large fare from this completely green foreigner. And he got it!

We first rode through the Legation Quarter, which has paved streets and its own wall surrounding it. As we left it, we came onto Hatamen Street. There were lots of people everywhere, selling their goods spread out on blankets on the sidewalk (the Chinese call them, jokingly, t'i t'ou pu tze – bend the head stores) or on little carts. There were no motor cars on the streets, only some bicycles and many rickshaws, all drawn by people and only occasionally a larger cart with a horse or donkey. And there, through the Hatamen gate, came a string of camels in their slow and majestic stride, carrying bags of coal. We turned the corner north at the Methodist Eye Hospital (where I was to work the last year of my time in Peking) and soon we were at Wenham Hall. I had seen quite a few beggars along the way and people in general were shabbily dressed, but everywhere one looked there were smiling, relaxed faces and they seemed to be telling each other jokes much of the time. Riding through the side streets, hutungs, I noticed that they were bordered by walls without windows on either side and only occasionally there was a small wooden door which was usually closed. If it was open, one could see a wall just inside this door, a little larger than the door itself, which obstructed the view of the inside yard. I found out later that this wall is there to prevent evil spirits, who are believed to go only straight, from entering the house, while people could, of course, walk around the wall on either side. This architectural trait of walls everywhere must have to do with the stress laid on privacy and the family system in the old China.

Even Wenham Hall, an American compound, had a wall around it, but there was a big gate and one could see in from the outside quite well. I was assigned a room and, after taking a shower (what a luxury in those days), I went straight to bed to catch up on my sleep. They woke me for dinner which was served in the common dining room. All the students were Chinese and I was a little ashamed to find that their English was very much better than mine – but they welcomed me cordially and helped me patiently to get acquainted. There was one other problem! I didn't know how to use chop sticks and there were no other utensils available. At the end of this slow dinner, I had mastered the art. Walking back to my room, I heard some familiar music and, following the sound, came to the open door of Steven Chang's room. He was the chief resident in medicine, proctor of Wenham Hall and a great lover of classical music. He was playing a good recording of

Tchaikovsky's Piano Concerto. I introduced myself and immediately liked him a lot because of his outgoing and friendly manner.

The next day, he walked with me the three blocks over to the Medical School Compound, where he introduced me to some of the key persons, mainly Miss Mary Ferguson, the Recorder and "Queen of the PUMC" as she was nicknamed. She was one of those superefficient, friendly American women, a missionary's daughter, who knew China and the workings of the PUMC inside out (recently she published an excellent book about the history of the PUMC which I cherish very much). I was really impressed with the place. It was built in a modified Chinese style in gray brick with green Chinese roofs, but inside looked just like any other modern American hospital or laboratory. One could see immediately that John D. Rockefeller, Jr. had not tried to save money when the project was conceived. Only the best and most expensive materials and equipment had been used. The curriculum of the school was patterned after Johns Hopkins and the idea was to train a small number of some highly qualified Chinese to be teachers at other Chinese medical schools (just the reverse of what the Chinese communists are trying to do now!) We had only about twenty-five students in each class and there were many more faculty members than students. When the school was started, most of the teachers were recruited from all over the world, usually top people. Gradually, as more and more Chinese advanced, they were taken into the faculty and, by the time I was there, only the heads of the departments were foreigners. There had been only one foreign student in all the seventeen years of the school's existence. I did not particularly cherish this privileged position because it demanded so much responsible performance and there was so much expected from me already.

I soon met Dr. Fortuyn, the Dutch Professor of Anatomy, who became like a father to me later on. I had the most trouble with biochemistry, because we had so little of this subject in Vienna and because it is a difficult subject for me in any case. The examiner and professor was the famous Dr. Hsien Wu (the Folin-Wu reaction was named after him) and I think I almost flunked that test. Otherwise, I did pretty well. My memory was good then and the motivation to study tremendous. Besides preparing for all the exams, I took Chinese lessons daily from a very clever teacher who did not speak a word of English. Experience had shown that this was the best way to learn the language – probably because it required really very clever teachers. I did not attempt to learn to write or read. I had enough with learning spoken Chinese, which was all the school required and I was in good company with 95% of the Chinese population who were illiterate. During the summer months, I got a nice job as house and dog sitter for a rich young Australian who went home, and this meant living in a beautiful quiet place with all my needs taken care of by a cook and two servants and having all the time to study – except for some walks with the smart German shepherd dog and occasional invitations to parties in the foreign colony. Little did I know that I was to meet my future wife at that very same place. September came and I had finally passed all my exams, including the Chinese, which consisted only of taking a history of a patient who fortunately was very smart and did not give me much trouble. He even knew his diagnosis, the Chinese word for which was familiar to me – he had malaria. Then trouble started elsewhere. My ulcer acted up badly and I had to spend two weeks in the hospital on a lousy sippy diet.

Now, finally, I had enough leisure time for reading and learning something about China and this strange new world into which I had been dumped. The PUMC, this little

American island, was not like home to me either. The American medical school system was very different from ours and I did struggle with the English, of course, but still as far as medicine goes, things were relatively familiar. The China outside our walls was quite another story, for which I was even less prepared. We had learned practically nothing about the Far East in school, except some geography and the general statement that China had one of the oldest of civilizations. There was a lot to be learned! I read as many books as I could get hold of and was eager to talk to people who had lived in China for a longer time in order to understand the present political situation. Japan had occupied and controlled almost half of China while Chiang Kai-shek, the hero and head of free China directed the defense from Chungking in the south west. I discovered Lin Yu-tang's and Pearl Buck's books and also Richard Wilhelm's translation of the Chinese classics (through his son, Helmut, who lived in Peking). It was also during this time that I first ran across Will Durant's *Story of Philosophy* and I have since grown old with him and his writings.

News from Japan was good. Mama had arrived safely with my grandparents and was living with Paul. Kurt had found a job as an accountant with an American movie firm in Tokyo. We heard from Papa every so often. Apparently he was not being bothered too much and was studying English very conscientiously – looking forward to joining us soon. I recuperated well under the care of Dr. Snapper, our Chief of Medicine. He had been the personal physician to the Queen of Holland before accepting the Professorship at the PUMC. I entered the fourth year class now as a regular student and struggled along with their strenuous requirements, but it was in retrospect a very happy and interesting year, except for our worries about the general situation in Europe and my particular concern for Papa. Hitler had invaded Poland on

September 1st and England had declared war, being bound by treaty, on September 3, 1939. The world was again engulfed in another murderous struggle, causing untold misery as it unfolded. Japan, as an Axis power, got into the mess too, and saw this as an opportunity to attack the French (Indochina), British (Malaya, Singapore) and Dutch (Indonesia) holdings in the Far East.

As a gesture of friendship for their Axis partners, the Germans, Japan stopped all immigration of Jewish refugees into Shanghai. The ones who were there were confined to a ghetto which made life very miserable for them. This move also eliminated Shanghai as an escape route for Papa! In Peking, there were so few refugees (about 10 souls) that the Japanese authorities didn't bother to pester us. Life in Peking changed very little at first. Members of the foreign colony whose country was at war with Germany (and Japan) were not interfered with in the beginning. They kept on going to their own parties and, in the International Peking Club, the Germans just did not mix with the others as freely as before. I was invited to parties of the US Embassy staff mostly and also to the outings that some of their young people made. We visited and explored the interesting sites outside the city like the Summer Palace, the Jade Fountain and the Western Hills on the weekends.

I got acquainted with a very nice language student from the British Embassy who gave me a fantastic present when he later left Peking – his British-made bicycle. This really gave me mobility to get to know the city and the country around it. He also introduced me to Hedda Hammer, a young German lady who was, as I found out later, a spy for the British. She was an outstanding photographer and had left Germany several years before, in protest against her Nazi infested family. Through her, I got a very good introduction to the old and the new China. She gave me many of her duplicate prints and some beautiful enlargements which I still keep in fond memory of her and China the way I remember it. She had an extraordinary gift for photographing people in their everyday life situations – smiles and happiness, humor and mischievousness, seriousness and sorrow, richness and poverty – they are all there. Her great book about old Peking with her unique pictures was published in 1985.[1] The wonderful pictures are now of historical value. Just one illustration of old Peking: An elderly gentleman taking his pet bird on a morning outing.

Through Hedda, I met another German lady who also could not care less about the mystique and laws of Nazism, even though she was married to a prominent Nazi who was attached to the German Embassy in Tokyo – Hanna Woidt. She was one of those liberated women of the early period before "women's lib," living with her dogs and her son from a previous marriage in rural Pao Ma Chang, about two miles outside the city walls. She obviously had lots of money and enjoyed helping lame ducks, like myself. Maybe this was her way of trying to make good for the crimes committed against the Jews in Germany. She was the one who bought me a cello (which I still have) when she heard that I played that instrument somehow, through her many acquaintances, she managed to get a quartet together. I'll never forget her, just for this reason – but there is, of course, another reason to always remember her. In 1942, she once invited Trude and me for dinner, trying to make a match. She had heard that I had been going with a Chinese lady doctor, Dr. Chang Eh, a resident in ophthalmology, and apparently wanted to get me out of that involvement! She also was very instrumental in bringing

---

[1] Morrison, Hedda, *A Photographer in Old Peking* (Hong Kong: Oxford Univ. Press, 1985)

Mama to Peking through her Japanese connections. In the same way that she helped me, she helped many others in need, but fate has not been as kind to her. She got divorced from her husband after the war, ending up alone in a tiny apartment on New York's East Side, almost crippled with arthritis. We have remained friends and maintained contact through all these years and I well know that she deserved better!

As I rotated through the various specialties during my fourth year, I felt most at home in the eye department. Not only had I had very intensive training in this field in Vienna under Professor Meller, but the PUMC eye clinic had been completely modeled after the Vienna clinic because the visiting professors were almost all from that school. They started with famous old Ernst Fuchs, later, von Sallmann, Pillat and Kronfeld. In all the other departments, things were done very differently from the way we had learned in Vienna. In general I found the American system far superior to our old one, because we students were so much more closely supervised and had more chance to discuss problems with our visiting staff doctors all the time. Of course, the ratio of student to staff was almost 1 to 1, while in Vienna it had been 100 to 1. We certainly wasted a lot of time in Vienna, where we had to plot our way without much help. My interest in ophthalmology was naturally enhanced by my friendship with Dr. Chang Eh, a second year resident in ophthalmology; she certainly played her part in my choosing that field as my specialty later on. Through her, I also got a much deeper insight into Chinese life and mentality and saw how little difference the color of the skin makes when it comes to being in love. After Pearl Harbor, at the end of 1941, when the PUMC had to close down, she left for free China and I never heard from her again. Rumor had it that she died of pneumonia.

Another unforgettable person of my Peking days was Father

Teilhard de Chardin. He frequently came to our Cenozoic Lab in the Anatomy Department where the skull of "Nellie," the famous Peking man, was kept. He had been instrumental in the excavation of the then oldest human fossil near Chu K'ou T'ien, west of Peking. The geological formation in which it had been found pointed to an age of about one million years. He and Dr. Weidenreich, a well-known German paleontologist, always had a great deal to discuss on their subject. He also often spent long hours talking to Mrs. Cowen, the secretary at the Institute, who was a very smart and charming lady with whom Father Teilhard loved to discuss religious and philosophical questions. Since I often visited, I did get a chance to listen in on some of these conversations. I did not know then that he was working on his book, *The Phenomenon of Man*, and I got only glimpses of his ideas in these discussions. He tried out his ideas on almost everyone who was willing to listen, in order to get a reaction. He was a very lively, enthusiastic and even entertaining person, intensely interested in his subject, very kind in his manners and could carry one along on his idealistic and metaphysical trips. Once I heard him give a talk entitled "Vie et Planet" at the French Embassy and I got a reprint of this paper afterwards. I was really impressed with the depth of his knowledge of science (it was my first serious contact with astronomy), his profound vision of the universe and the mystical interpretation of its purpose. Had I realized then what a great man he was, I would have made more of an effort to know him better personally, instead of having to catch up on his ideas later in life. He has become a guiding light in my own view on life. I consider myself fortunate to have known him "in the flesh."

I saw him last in 1951, when we passed through Paris on our way to the United States. He was staying at a Jesuit monastery in a tiny simple room, almost a cell, with one table, two chairs and an iron rod bed – and many books, of course. He was very kind and seemed happy to see me. The old man was quite depressed because he had just received news from Rome that the Pope had refused publication of his book, because the ideas expressed in it did not quite go along with the teachings of the church. He died not too long afterwards, and then his friends published all of his works and started almost a cult around him. He has given hope and guidance to millions of people with his mystical and optimistic interpretation of evolution and in showing that a synthesis between science and religion was possible. In the meantime, the church has, without much fanfare, taken him back into her fold, digesting his ideas without apology for the misery caused to him when he was exiled to China. At least he did not suffer the fate of Galileo Galilei!

And then there was lively, happy and boisterous Tony Freeman, the American language student who befriended me. He was an excellent musician, played practically every instrument, and was always the life of every party. He had started his diplomatic career in Peking, was evacuated at the outbreak of the war in the Pacific, came back with a most charming wife (Phyllis) and a baby, right after the war and took my first application for immigration to the United States. When we left Peking, he was the one who took us to the train station in his Jeep. We could have never made the train with Marianne, then a three-month-old baby, with all the junk we had.

In the fall of 1940 (I was then taking my internship) I received a cable from Hapag (a German shipping agency) with the ominous message, "Arrange immediately entrance permit for your father." We had been cut off from Europe since Hitler had invaded Russia earlier that year and had thus interrupted the trans-Siberian communication line. This cable was the first sign from Papa in many months and it sounded like a desperate cry for help, help which I did not know how to give. I immediately got in touch with Mrs. Woidt to see if she could, through her Japanese connections, arrange some kind of entry permit for him, but she was not successful. I wrote to Mama in Japan to try over there, but nothing came of that either. It was a miserable situation. In a way, I was fortunate to be so very busy with my duties as an intern that I could not worry all day long, but in the early morning hours, when everything always looks blacker than normal, the feeling of helplessness was distressing. It seemed so unreal that in our corner of the world nothing much seemed to change, while we knew that Europe was torn apart in the war. The Japanese occupation army became a little more obnoxious with the Blitzkrieg advances of the Germans, but otherwise life went on as usual.

In June 1941 our class had the traditional graduation ceremony in cap and gown – everybody smiling and happy. How I wished that Papa could have been there! I was truly grateful that fate, in the guise of Mr. Rockefeller, had made it possible for me to finish medical school in spite of everything.

During my intern year, I had, as required, written my thesis. I chose as a subject, "Diabetic Retinopathy in the Chinese" which showed already my leaning toward ophthalmology, so that when the time came to apply for a residency, it naturally was ophthalmology. And when I was accepted and started to work in the eye department, I really had a great time. Everything somehow came very easily and I found it fascinating and rewarding to settle down to a field that I really enjoyed. We had no foreign professor – Dr. Kronfeld had left the year before – but Dr. Luo, as Acting Head, was an inexhaustible fountain of knowledge and loved to teach, which made up a hundred times for his relative ineptness in surgery. "How long does it take before one sees any details in the eye ground?" was my question when I first tried to use the ophthalmoscope.

Retinoscopy seemed like magic that took me a long time to really catch on to. I am always amazed how fast our residents here learn to handle our rather complicated instruments. It took me a long time to be sure of my observations, but I always enjoyed observing fine details. Even today, I sometimes get carried away in watching, for instance, on the slit lamp microscope, clumps of red blood cells rushing through a conjunctival vessel. The patient may think I am finding something terribly wrong with his eyes, because I take so much time looking – while I am actually enjoying nature at work. I liked the exactness that is the hallmark in ophthalmology, where one usually can see directly what one is talking about and does not have to guess or infer indirectly, as in Internal Medicine.

Actually, during my internship I liked Internal Medicine too, and was pretty good at guessing and in making a diagnosis. I remember two unusual cases in which I, the little intern, made the right diagnosis and the visiting physician did not. One was a huge pancreatic cyst that presented like a massive ascites; the other a subacute bacterial endocarditis that I diagnosed from a petechial hemorrhage in the con-junctiva. I had trouble with the parasitic and subtropical infectious diseases that were all new to me. Except for the very heavy workload as an intern, (we had to do all our routine blood, urine and stool examinations ourselves and had to write the most elaborate histories, often until 2:00 a.m.) it was a happy time, and ophthalmology was even better. But unfortunately it did not last!

December 7, 1941 – Pearl Harbor! We woke up in the morning and Japanese soldiers were everywhere in the hospital and at the gates. We could not believe the news! They allowed us to continue to take care of the patients in the hospital, but the OPD was closed and no new admissions were allowed. Nobody knew what was going to happen. One morning, I was pulled out of bed at 4:00 a.m. by a Japanese soldier and taken to their headquarters for interrogation. I had a clear conscience and could not understand what they wanted from me. I was interviewed in a little cell for hours by an army officer through an interpreter, and it took ages before I finally realized what they were after.

Apparently, they had been watching my mail to Kurt and Mama in Japan very carefully, and thought I was a spy. Their suspicion was based on two ridiculous bits of evidence that had been blown completely out of proportion by their paranoid fear of spies. I had never posted my letter myself, but had made little pencil marks indicating the amount of postage on the envelope where the stamp was to be placed, so that the servant in our dorm knew what the postage should be when he mailed the letter. These little marks, because they were hidden under the stamps, were, for the Japanese Intelligence, a secret code that had to be cracked! When they showed me some of the envelopes that they had collected (I had wondered why several of my letters had not arrived) with those numbers on them, they were a little puzzled (and I hope embarrassed) by my obvious and simple explanation.

The other big alibi was a sentence in one of my letters to Mama where I wrote something like "es war alles für die Katz"(it was all for the cat – colloquial for "to no avail"). They pestered me for almost an hour because I could not tell them who the "Katz" was. It is amazing how paranoia can distort a person's thinking processes. After I had passed this hurdle, it was about 2:00 p.m. By then, the interrogating army officer began to loosen up a bit, took a nice big apple that was lying on his table, cut it in half and shared it with me. I am sure not all of his interrogations ended that cordially. I had been lucky again.

A few days after that, the PUMC had to be evacuated by order of the Japanese military. Dr. Fortuyn was so kind as to ask me to stay with them and I accepted, happily. I could not have gone to a better place than their peaceful little house where I was accepted lovingly, but without fuss. Somehow, I heard that Dr. Pi, a Chinese ophthalmologist with his own small eye hospital, was looking for an assistant. He had been a very well thought of associate professor at the PUMC years back and I was very glad when I got the job, because I hoped to be able to learn something from him, besides earning my bread (without butter). He put me in charge of his charity clinic, where I saw about 20 patients each morning – mostly external diseases. This was fine except for the fact that Dr. Pi never explained anything to me when I had any questions. Fortunately, he had a small ophthalmologic library which I discovered by accident and which he let me use, reluctantly, so that I could read up by myself and learn. When he did surgery, I was allowed to assist and this I enjoyed, but again, I had trouble getting him to explain to me the various indications, types of procedures, pitfalls and complications, etc.

His wife, a fat little lady with a sweet smile, was much kinder. She was the one who would try to supplement the subsistence level diet with little morsels of meat and other delicacies, and even invited me occasionally to eat with the family in their dining room where better class Chinese food was served. This better class food was a far cry from what we here eat in good Chinese restaurants. I always ate with the nurses in a little room behind the kitchen. Breakfast consisted of shi fan (watery rice) with chien t'sai (salted vegetable bits) and for lunch, we usually had steamed buns with fried or cooked vegetables. At times we had soup. I remember the menu because it was the same every day and I very soon started buying myself eggs and put them in the shi fan to make it more nourishing and tasty, and also to keep my ulcer a little more at peace. In the evenings, I ate at the Fortuyn's – simple, but good. My monthly salary was about the equivalent of $10.00 – which I used mostly to buy ophthalmic instruments that were brought by peddlers – all stolen goods from the PUMC. I even found a small trial case, which later, when I had my own office in Peking, became the bread-winning tool. A few years ago, I gave it to a Chinese friend, Dr. Ding, who was going back from here to Hong Kong to practice. So it returned to its source.

The Fortuyns were exceptionally nice people. We often sat together in the evenings for hours discussing philosophical subjects and frequently read aloud chapters from Will Durant's *Story of Civilization* that had just appeared, and of which I had found a copy at the flea market bookstore. But their time to depart drew close. As Dutch citizens, they were evacuated to South Africa at first, from there he went to teach at the medical school in Surinam. He left me some of his library, mostly the German classics, which I still have. I was then invited to stay with Mr. Plant, a German Jewish art collector and dealer who had lived in China for over twenty years. He had come originally as a journalist and became so interested in Chinese art and curios that he turned completely to that field for a living. He had a huge hall full of statues and other art objects, and he offered me one of his beautiful Chinese beds (k'ang), that he figured would not be sold the next day, to sleep on. It was not a very cozy place, even though I was surrounded by art objects, and sometimes when I woke in the middle of the night, I got a little frightened at first with all those silent ghostlike statues around me, until I realized where I was.

In the meantime in Japan, Paul and Mama had both been put into jail as suspected spies. Kurt had left the year before for the United States, Grandpapa had died the year previously from diabetic gangrene of the foot, and so there were only three of them. Now, only Grandmama was free. Mama got so desperate in prison with all the interrogation and the hopelessness of the situation that she tried to kill herself by cutting her wrists. This scared her torturers (they apparently still had some respect for white skin then) and she was let out. This was after two months in prison. Paul came out a little later. They had been living in Hiroshima, because that is where Paul had found another job. After they were free, they all moved back to Yokohama. I guess they had to stay in jail so long because it took all this time for the world-shaking secrets, revealed in *my* interview, to reach Japan and convince everybody that they really had not been spying.

Toward the end of 1942 I was summoned to the Peking German Embassy to surrender my passport because my citizenship had been revoked (see appendix).

One day Mrs. Woidt decided that Mama must come and live with me in Peking. It was a very obvious thought from a strictly human point of view, but how could I hope to make this possible as a stateless refugee in a country at war and paranoid about foreign spies! But she had her own ideas and, mainly, her own connections. Introduced by a Japanese lady friend of hers, she arranged an appointment with a high Japanese army official. The three of us went there together and presented the case in the typically polite manner. Not knowing Japanese, I could not follow the conversation, of course, but somehow she must have convinced the officer of the merit of our plea, because I got a travel permit for Mama. When I asked the Japanese lady afterwards how she had done that, she explained that it was really quite simple because the man understood that a mother and her son should be together and that this took precedence over restrictive wartime travel regulations. I'll never forget this in my evaluation of Japanese culture!

So I began to look for a place for us to stay and found a small three room house which used to be the Kan Men Di's (gatekeeper's) abode in a larger family compound. All the members of this once prosperous household had left for Free China and only the old mother had stayed behind to supervise the place. She rented out part of the compound to support herself while waiting out the war and the return of her family. This was a very common situation in Peking then, because so many upper-class Chinese had fled to the interior when the Japanese started taking over the country in 1937 where Chiang Kai-shek directed the resistance. In those days Chiang was the great hero of the country and China had very close and friendly ties to America, which was helping them in their war efforts against the invaders (Burma Road, etc.). I myself felt very pro-Nationalist Chinese in those days and detested the Japanese occupation army. The above story of Mama's permit, therefore, was an all the more pleasant surprise.

Mama came over around Christmas, 1942. With the help of friends, I had fixed up this primitive apartment – which consisted mainly in repapering the windows and white-washing the walls. I got a heating stove from somewhere (I almost died one night from carbon monoxide poisoning) and even dug a hole in the corner of the kitchen room that connected under the bottom of the house foundation wall with a similar hole on the street side. Over this I put a wooden box (Donner Büchse) as a toilet seat. In this way the waste disposal problem was solved. Peking had practically no sewer system in those days. Human waste was picked up to be used as fertilizer in the field by men going around with a large wooden bucket strapped to their back and a big ladle with a long handle to empty the cesspools, or simply to pick up usable refuse from the side streets that were used as open toilets by the people. They had an uncanny way of emptying their ladle into the bucket by swinging it over their shoulder without soiling themselves. This system must have supported the men who did this job, besides being ecologically very sound. One could not say that it was very sanitary, since it made it possible for many parasites to happily follow their life cycle for thousands of years.

There also was no water in the house – it was brought in once a day by the water carrier who had his special signal, consisting of the squeaky sound of the big wheels of his cart. He emptied his two buckets full into our large earthen bowl standing in the courtyard. Cooking was done on the ubiquitous small open portable stove that used coal balls made out of coal dust and clay. These stoves had to be lit outside and were carried into the kitchen only after the coal was burning red and no more suffocating fumes were rising up. It was a far cry from a modern kitchen, but Mama managed very well and I was happy to see her positive approach to the situation. She was obviously content to be with me and run my house.

It was a really primitive place, but we spent many happy hours there with friends visiting all the time and the feeling of being together in those uncertain times. I had met Trude a few months before Mama came and we had frequently gone together on our weekend bicycle trips, always with the same gang consisting of two or three Wang girls (Ui Didi, Billa), Lo (Loewental, author of the book, *The Jews in China*) and Olly Willner. Sometimes, Dr. Weiss joined us. Then, Trude was staying with her host family, the Haasens, who had been old friends of her family in Germany. Her father had originally been in the German diplomat service, left that job because of his "non Aryan" wife, studied theology and eventually moved with his family to Geneva, Switzerland. There he started a refugee department of the World Council of Churches. Trude soon found Switzerland too small for her youthful, enterprising spirit and managed to leave via Siberia for Peking, just before WW II started in 1939.

I left Dr. Pi soon after Mama arrived (one year of that was enough) and joined the Catholic French Hospital. I hoped to make a little more money there and be able to pay for our rent and food. It was a change for the better, but it meant a constant hassle with the extremely stingy Mère Supérieure. The inflation was so rapid that the salary negotiated for at the beginning of each month was worth only two thirds of that by the end, so an occasional bonus of a sack of flour was worth gold. Again, I was in charge of the charity clinic for which I got my small salary, but I was allowed to see private patients and charge them separately. It was a struggle, but we survived, and looking back, these seem to have been happier times than the present one where we have everything we could wish for materially, but struggle with disappointments in our close human relationships and in the idealist expectation for this world.

Of course, we were also young and just then, my relationship to Trude slowly but steadily grew into a deeper commitment, and the general world situation was such that there was hope for a victory for the allies some day. At least, the enemy was clearly defined and, even if he was still winning most of the time, there were forces gaining strength against him with America in the war. There was hope, confidence and a strong belief that the "good guys" would eventually win. Today we really don't know the enemy, there is confusion, disillusionment, uncertainty and no clearcut goal towards which we can look with confidence – except, maybe, a supernatural one.

One gets very edgy sitting in an eddy of the mainstream of events with only scant and distorted information on the progress of the war and waiting year after year for a favorable turn of events. I remember many talks with a friend (Loewental, author of *The Jews in China*.),who also was very restless, about how we could travel to Free China through the mountainous area of North China on foot until we came into unoccupied territory. It was a crazy idea and I am glad we did not attempt it. It would have meant traveling through communist territory first and they would never have let us pass.

We were curious about the communists, the so called 8th Route Army, who were more or less in control outside the Japanese occupied zone, which extended about fifteen miles around the city and along the railroads. They rarely did anything to harass the Japanese. They were too smart (and too weak) for that. They consolidated themselves in the North-western Provinces with Yunnan as capital and tried to indoc-trinate the peasantry in their territory. Even at that time they knew that their real enemy was not Japan, but their own Nationalist Chinese brethren and, therefore, also the Ameri-cans. It was in their best interests, accordingly, not to interfere much with the Japanese because they were fighting their battle against Chiang. All this I could not understand. To me, Chinese were Chinese, communist or not; they should want to get the invading Japanese out of the country. Only after the end of the war, when the outposts of the Japanese army were withdrawn and the communists moved closer in, did we see anti-American slogans smeared on the walls of the villages that we used to visit on our Sunday bike trips about six to eight miles out of town. I was baffled. Why should Chinese express anti-American feelings when America was helping them win the war?

We actually did meet the communists some time before the end of the war at Pater Maas' temple/resthouse. Pater Maas was a German priest, the son of an innkeeper in the Rhein-land, who lived way out in the hills just beyond the Japanese controlled area in an old Buddhist temple that the church had acquired. He was growing grapes for their winery out there, besides his main occupation of saving his soul – and maybe those of some local converts and some of his retreat visitors from town. There were some less orthodox things he did, because he was not an ordinary man. In the tradition of his father, he ran a very comfortable little vacation station where good food was served and people could get a good rest over a long weekend or longer. He had a kind pink face and snow white hair with a little goatee, and his company was very pleasant. Trude and I visited there several times. It was about a fifteen-mile bicycle ride on dirt roads, but always worth it.

The first time we went there we learned that he also ran a little dispensary to which some of the guerrillas from the 8th Route Army would come after dark for medicines or to have their wounds treated. So we had an opportunity to meet them. They felt fairly safe with him and he with them. He gladly provided them with medical care and they, in turn, left him in peace or, actually, protected him. During the day they with-drew into the hills; in the evening they would come down and mix with the villagers to indoctrinate them. I was amazed at those characters. They were dressed like ordinary peasants, but had their guns. Most of them were young people, usually sons of city intellectuals, who really led a very Spartan life, full of idealism, tough and purposeful, smart and dedicated – so different from the young Chinese that I had met so far in Peking, particularly my former classmates at the PUMC. We were so impressed by them that from then on I always took medicine along for them when we visited Pater Maas.

On one occasion, we saw even more of them. It was shortly before the end of the war at the period of the pilgrimage to Miao Feng Shan, a famous temple some distance beyond Pater Maas' temple. The communists allowed people from the city to travel there and used the occasion to show the city folks what they were doing. A small group of us went too, and promptly came to a village where the circus was on. The main street was a big bazaar, but not with goods. They had stands with propaganda writings and many, many large pictures and photos of Russian and Chinese communist heroes and of famous buildings in Moscow, factories, machinery, etc., etc. They also had built a simple stage, and we were urgently invited to see the show on our way back from the temple. Since it was getting late by the time we returned, we tried to get out of this invitation, but they gently insisted and took us aside into a house and tried to talk us into staying. Finally, I explained to them that I had to be back the next morning to see my patients and then they let us go. It was a narrow escape. They could easily have kept us there by force, particularly after they knew what a useful profession I had, but they didn't.

Everyone admired the heroic resistance that the Russian people put up against the Nazi war machine. Even our neighbors, an elderly White Russian couple, who naturally detested the communists, got very patriotic and, under their influence, I decided to study Russian with them in my spare time. I did not get very far, unfortunately. In those days, I met a Polish ophthalmologist priest, who was visiting Peking for a few weeks. I got very interested in the work he was doing in an area about two-hundred miles south of Peking. He worked out of a small mission hospital in Kai-feng and had established several rural dispensaries for which he had trained local

Chinese "medics," mainly in recognizing and treating eye diseases. He made the rounds of these dispensaries every two to three months, seeing the complicated cases and doing the necessary eye surgery. I thought this was a great idea, very imaginative for that time. Now I realize that this was the first awakening of my later humanitarian dreams and efforts and made Albert Schweitzer's work so exciting to me when I first discovered him later on.

On September 3, 1944, Trude and I got married at the Haasen's house. The night before was the big dinner to which several of our bicycling friends were invited and, of course, Mama was there. I had no idea how many courses there would be, and Trude had not warned me, so I started filling up on the first one, which must have been very good. When we came to the third, I could not have another bite and became the laughing stock of the party. There also was much laughter about a telegram that Trude's parents had sent that gave in short funny rhymes, her life's history. I only remember, "Unverdrossen, Bock geschossen." The marriage ceremony was performed by Pastor Lehmann, the German minister for the Peking community. It was simple and well done and our sermon title was "Der Eine trage des Andern Last." (One should carry the other's burden.) Then the official papers, obtained at the police station, were signed by the witnesses, and that was it. Not quite, though, since now Trude, being married to a stateless person, legally lost her German citizenship and was required to relinquish her passport. She herself had no objection to that; but Willy Haas, the former diplomat, who knew more about these things, was dead set against it. He felt responsible for Trude's safety and we had quite a hassle with him, but eventually Trude did turn in this valuable paper, accepting fate in these matters – as I had done earlier in Zagreb.

We spent a very nice honeymoon in Pei Tai Ho, a coastal

summer resort north of Tientsin. There were beautiful beaches and hills for long walks and charming Chinese villages to visit. Our favorite place was a tiny restaurant, actually just a little shack, where they had excellent fish. We would watch the cook, a gentle old man, prepare it, adding all the many different spices and always giving us – "Ta Kuo' erl Di[2]"). Trude did not get jealous of my catching butterflies and it was a happy time all the way around. Returning to Peking, we moved to another apartment, where I also fixed up one room to examine patients. Mama stayed at our old place and soon Paul joined her, since Grandmama had died and his job in Japan was finished. Both my grandparents are buried together in the cemetery on the bluff in Yokohama, a large pine tree growing over their grave.

Peking was a beautiful city and its surroundings had a special charm, too. One of our favorite places was the Temple of Heaven in the South City. In the huge inner walled quadrangle were three temples in a row, in the middle a small one with a beautiful cobalt blue roof surrounded by the famous round whispering wall. If one person was standing on the inside of this wall and whispered in a very low voice, another could hear it about fifty feet away, half way around the circumference. To the north and south of it were the two large temples, both built in three superimposed round marble terraces, almost like a layered birthday cake, with marble railings around the border. The top platform, was about 120 feet across, the bottom about 200 feet. The North Temple, the one commonly seen on pictures, had a tall superstructure, a round red building with a blue roof, all very ornately painted. The inside was just one huge round hall with red pillars supporting the roof structure and the usual Buddha figure. It was much too decorated for my taste.

---

[2] Especially large helpings.

The South Temple was the one I really liked. There, the emperor used to perform the yearly ceremonies. It was without any building on top of the terraces, just the open marble platform with the marble railings and the four staircases leading up to it from north, south, east and west. I was taken by the concept of openness to the sky for worshiping heaven. Another uplifting feature was the four entrance gates, which were shaped out of very tall marble pillars extending upward beyond the wide cross bar, and seemed to penetrate above it through a cloud, again carved out of white marble. I got inspired by many of these sights and painted quite a few pictures, of which we kept only a few. The rest I gave away to friends to whom I felt grateful for kindnesses they had shown me. Trude likes some of them because they brought back happy memories and also because they were painted on the site and not copied from slides. I wish, though, we had had color films to record those striking colors, particularly the old imperial buildings with their brilliantly gold-colored roofs.

A very favorite pastime was to go window shopping in the special districts outside Hata Men. There were the silk street, the pewter street, the brass street, the silver street, the jade street and so on and on. Trude had a special place where she always got honey, which was all we had for sweetening because the cost of sugar was out of reach. She made friends with the owner there and, one day, came home with a painting he had made for her while she waited there watching him do it. It was fun to watch the Chinese going to these places, not with the idea of buying anything, but just to look around and bargain for the fun of it. It was better entertainment than TV! We learned their ways and had fun too, even buying a few things here and there. One thing I remember in particular was a nice jade necklace which I bought for Trude as an engagement present. Unfortunately, she lost it on one of our bicycle outings to Pao Ma Chang.

About a year before the end of the war we saw, for the first time, an American plane flying very high over Peking. Actually all one could see was the double streak of white vapor. It was an electrifying event! Our friends were coming! Our morale jumped 300% and people talked of nothing else for days. Sometime later we heard planes again without actually seeing any, but the rumor went around that several Japanese planes had been destroyed in a bombing attack on the airfield. More and more reports came through about the defeats of the German armies in Russia and North Africa and also the terrible bombing of cities in Europe. It was hard to imagine all the suffering that must have gone on in Europe and in the South Pacific while we were sitting in relative peace and comfort. Then came the Normandy landing in June 1944, with the allies establishing a beachhead with terrific losses but succeeding in breaking the defenses and invading France. Fortunately Paris was not destroyed, because the German commander there did not obey Hitler's orders, but followed his own better judgment and evacuated the city before the US troops came in.

It took another eleven months after that before Germany finally collapsed as the two armies, from the east and west, closed in and met on the River Elbe. The worst destruction happened at the very end and it must have been real hell for the people. Three months later the atomic bomb fell on Hiroshima and two days later on Nagasaki. I wonder how long the Japanese, who were already exhausted and demoralized by three years of war, would have gone on fighting without this monstrous weapon – and whether President Truman's justification for dropping the bomb, namely to save American lives by avoiding the casualties from an invasion of Japan proper, was really valid. The fact is that the bomb was used on cities (with all the psychological consequences) and that the Japanese were so stunned that they surrendered. The occupation army in Peking didn't know what to do. They were there walking the streets, still in uniform (they had no other clothes, I guess), carrying their guns because there was no one to disarm them. Only a month later, the first US Marines landed in Tientsin and came up to Peking to take over. It took another two months before, finally, the first contingent of Nationalist Chinese soldiers were flown in from the south in US planes.

By that time I was working at the Methodist Eye Hospital, where we had a very interesting clinic. We lived, at first, in an apartment above the clinic and Trude didn't feel too much at ease looking down in the courtyard every morning on the forty to sixty patients with their running eyes, who had lined up for examination and treatment. Later, we got a house in the mission compound, which was a little more civilized and private.

Communication resumed with Europe, mostly through Trude's parents, and we found out that Papa had died in Vienna about the time of Pearl Harbor in December 1941. The only consolation was to know that he at least had not been deported to some of the Polish concentration camps and that Bamer and Peperl had both seen him in fairly good condition not long before he died. Lislott had managed to leave England during the Blitz and had joined Kurt in the United States. She went to college at Mt. Holyoke, probably with the help of Kurt's wife, Felicia. The overwhelming news from Europe was horror and tragedy. What insanity! What waste! Tony Freeman returned to the US Embassy in Peking, and with his help Mama got on the first evacuation ship, a US destroyer, which came to Tientsin to pick up the American prisoners of war from North China. She left early in the summer of 1946 to join Kurt in Berkeley.

On September 27, 1946 Marianne was born at the German Hospital, delivered by my good friend and former Chief Resident in OB at the PUMC, Tien Shui P'ing. I was, of course, allowed to be present and I still remember how we both sat there, waiting for things to happen "like a cat in front of a mouse hole." Trude felt well enough to think that this was very funny. She did extremely well, contrary to Mrs. Woidt's fears. The poor lady told me afterwards that she did not sleep all night because she worried about Trude. She really expected Trude to have a lot of trouble because of her polio and felt responsible for the whole affair because she considered herself the matchmaker. This went a little too far for me. Marianne was not exactly beautiful. She had long black hair and a red face and her nose was all bent to the right side. I joked that this was Dr. Tien's fault because his nose was similarly bent, but to the left. Only his was permanent! At that time we had some pet rabbits who had had darling little furry babies the week before. A few days after Marianne was born, I took one of those babies with me when I visited Trude in the hospital to show her how cute they were compared with our daughter. She has never forgiven me this joke.

We had put in our application with the UNNRA representative and were now waiting for a chance to leave. Nobody knew when there would be a ship going to Shanghai from where we had booked for the beginning of February 1947 on a French liner, *Champolion*. We tried to be ready, but nothing happened. Christmas came around and we even got a tree and decorated it. Then, on the 22nd of December, we got notice to leave for Tientsin, where an evacuation boat was supposed to depart on the 26th. I worked almost day and night to get things packed and crated for the ocean voyage, and there was not much chance to celebrate Christmas. Still, on the last morning, I had to run out at 6:00 a.m. to find another suitcase for our remaining junk. Our train was to leave at 8:00 a.m. If Tony had not picked us up with his Embassy Jeep, we would never have made it. As it was, we barely got on the last car as the train started to pull out. It was an exhausting affair. Since

Trude could not nurse Marianne because of her breast infection in October, I had constructed a small alcohol stove for heating the formula and when the time came to feed the baby, I tried it out and almost set the train on fire with the stupid thing. Marianne survived it. We arrived in Tienstsin and stayed, as previously arranged, at Dr. Bruell's hospital. He was an old Austrian doctor who had kindly invited us to use one of his hospital rooms in transit. Nobody could imagine, however, that this transit would last three weeks! Why did we have to leave Peking in such a hurry? But we almost enjoyed the time for relaxing and we got to know the Bruells and Tientsin a little better. I went to the docks daily to find out what was going on and even found our ship – an old LST (Landing Ship for Tanks) but nobody knew for sure when we were going to sail.

Finally we were told to board the ship. We happened to be among the privileged ones assigned to the crew's quarters on either side of the ship. There were nine or twelve bunks in each, always three on top of each other, and there were four or five berths in a row. We were in the last berth and had to go through all the others to get to ours. There were no windows, like in a submarine, and it was really a spooky place; not made for people with claustrophobia. But it was heaven compared to where most people were put, namely in the huge hold of the ship that was fitted for tanks, not humans. There were about four to five hundred people stacked in there like sardines. They had to produce their own heat. January is very cold in North China. I have no idea where they ate or where they had their toilets, but they were amazingly content to get this first opportunity to travel to Shanghai. I guess it all depends on how badly you want something and what you expect from a given situation in life, whether you can put up with it or not. I don't know what happened to them when the flat bottomed ship started to roll as we sailed around the tip of Shan-Tung in a moderate storm.

In our little berth, everybody was seasick except Marianne, who was laughing away. The more the ship bounced around, the more she seemed to enjoy it. The food was not bad, but most people couldn't eat. I was not too badly off. Usually I went for meals with my neighbor, a White Russian, Mr. Ostrovsky, who did not feel too bad either. Often, however, I vomited soon after meals and had to go back for more food. Trude was out of commission, so I had to change Marianne's diapers as well as take care of her – and Mrs. Ostrovsky – who was convinced she was going to die. Finally, I gave her a shot of morphine, the only thing I had with me, and "saved her life." With all the throwing up, the smell in our berth was pretty bad, but otherwise the whole scene was rather funny and we all made it alive to Shanghai.

Return to Europe

There was another three weeks wait in Shanghai before we got on the *SS Champolion*, where we had more decent, separate accommodations. Trude was busy with Marianne, preparing formula, washing diapers and watching her grow. In Saigon, we both went ashore to visit the botanical garden, but otherwise she did not dare to leave the ship. In Ceylon, which already had its independent status within the British empire, we were not allowed to land in Colombo because of a boycott of the harbor workers against the French as a colonial power in Indochina. So we landed in the tiny French colony of Pondicherry, on the east coast of India, which as far as I was concerned, was only good for catching butterflies. I still have them.

During our stay in Shanghai, somebody had given me a book about Albert Schweitzer, which I was reading now with the greatest interest. There was a hero figure in medicine, impressive enough to be worth imitating. What I had admired in the Polish priest ophthalmologist who worked in Kai-feng was here done on a much wider scale by an idealist – a philosopher and humanitarian with a real practical sense. He certainly has influenced my thinking; all my later striving to work in underprivileged areas, just for the love of it, goes back to my exposure to Schweitzer's ideas.

In my berth, I was together with three rabbis who were on their way to Palestine. They spent most of their time praying and checking out their food. There was, of course, no kosher food on the ship, so they were severely restricted in their diet and did not eat in the dining room. They brought bread to the berth, cut it in very thin slices and, holding it against the light, looked for insects in it. I guess mealworms are not exactly kosher. I thought they had a miserable life, but not so when they returned to the ship after visiting the Jewish community in Djibouti, where we could also go ashore. They were radiant with joy because they had found a very active Jewish congregation who observed all the orthodox laws to the letter and they had been invited to really fill up on kosher food! I regretted that I could not communicate more with them, because they spoke only Hebrew. They were very nice otherwise and never minded a bit when I washed Marianne's diapers in our sink, because of a water shortage in Trude's cabin.

We landed in Marseille on March 4, 1947, where friends of the Freudenbergs, Trude's parents, picked us up and had found accommodations for us before proceeding to Geneva by train. How beautiful Europe was! After seeing all these years the browns, grays and yellows of the Chinese scenery and, particularly after the desert around the Red Sea and the Suez Canal, it was obvious why Europe was called the "Green Continent." I loved those neat villages with their little red roofed houses and the churches everywhere – the wooded hills and big meadows and the higher mountains in the background. It was really exciting. We did not notice too much destruction – from the train, at least.

In Geneva, we were met by Trude's parents, who were as nice as I had pictured them from all I had heard, especially Vater. They were happy to have Trude back, to see their first grandchild and, I think, to meet their son-in-law. They had fixed up two rooms in their fourth floor apartment on the Ave. de Miremont, with a beautiful view over the valley of the Arve River and the Saleve Mountain ridge. It was great to get a little feeling of home again and be so warmly welcomed. It was also nice to live in this well organized and civilized country, in one of its most interesting cities. But then, Marianne came down with a bad case of whooping cough which she apparently had picked up on the ship. She developed an abscess in her left neck gland, which Dr. Bamater had to incise and I still remember the scene in our bedroom very well. How seemingly uncomplicated medical care was then!

Through Bamater, who had been a favorite assistant of Trude's Uncle Ernst, Professor of Pediatrics in Basel, and also a good friend of Franceschetti, the Professor of Ophthalmology in Geneva, I got a chance to work at the university eye clinic as an observer. What I had always hoped for in the years in China, where I considered myself a self-taught ophthalmologist, namely to get some more supervised training in my specialty, was here! Franceschetti was a dynamo of a person, a brilliant clinician, a kind pater familias to all his assistants and an inspiring teacher who made a deep impression on me. Not for nothing is his photograph the only one on my office desk. He seemed to like me but he was unable at that time to offer me a paid position. Fortunately, Trude found a secretarial job which contributed some to our upkeep.

The possibility for our immigration to the United States seemed in the nebulous future, since it depended on the oversubscribed Austrian quota. The US Consul in Zurich was completely noncommittal as to when it might come up. Two years? Five years? Besides, we both began to feel a little uneasy at times because Mutter, in her frequent need for a scapegoat, unfortunately had picked me. So I became more and more convinced that I should see whether it would be possible to resettle in Austria. Vater, in his refugee work with the World Council of Churches, had heard that Mrs. Krueger, a field worker of the American Brethren Church, was going to Vienna and was looking for someone to accompany her. It was obvious that I was the one to travel with her. Marianne was just beginning to become like a little person and I was not too happy to leave Trude and her behind, but I knew they were well taken care of and I knew that I had to make a start getting my feet on the ground.

Austrian Interlude

I will never forget the impressions from this trip. We drove and could, therefore, see so much more of the country and the people. The contrast between untouched and orderly Switzerland and Austria was shocking and apparent the moment we crossed the border into Vorarlberg. There was not so much actual destruction from bombing in the western provinces, except around the train stations in the cities; but the desolate poverty of the people and their depressed appearance was pitiful. This got worse the farther east we went and was devastating in Linz. Salzburg had also been pretty badly hit, but mostly the railroads; the historical sites had not been destroyed. Linz had been a major industrial town and apparently got heavy air raids. Vienna was not any better. This was two years after the end of the war.

Of course, the train stations were leveled and in their neighborhoods very few houses were standing. In the inner city, the destruction was really the worst. The Nazi army had withdrawn along the main thoroughfare, the Kärntnerstrasse (Vienna's main shopping street), from the incoming Russian troops and had burned everything down. The Opera and St. Stephan's Cathedral, the symbol of Vienna, were completely burned out. The steeple of the latter remained. The roof had fallen in and the famous big bell, the "Pummerin," had melted in the heat into blobs of bronze. But even worse was the misery of the people. Of course, I saw the poorest of the poor, whom Mrs. Krueger was attending – all refugees that had lost everything fleeing from the Russian army, German-speaking folks from the Eastern countries and Austria who were now stranded in camps in and around Vienna. Mrs. Krueger was excellent. I remember a talk she gave in German to a large group of them and how she managed to boost their morale and give them hope for the future again.

I stayed at Carl's flat where Paul, who had come back from China a few months earlier, had found temporary shelter also. It happened to be in the same house that Nistler lived in and I was very happy to see them all again. Nistler welcomed me with his old cordiality and urged me to stay and get a start in Vienna. He was again back in his old job as a sleeping car conductor, but I found him very much aged. He must have suffered a great deal in the concentration camp where he had spent almost two years. I did not realize then that he had only a few more months to live! Paul was trying to pick up his old connections to start the safety lock business again, which was quite a detective job in itself, because very few people could be found where they used to be and many had vanished altogether. But he eventually managed to get the business going again.

I went to the eye clinic and started to work there free, trying to pick up what I could and making contacts. It was a depressing place with all these many patients and completely insufficient supplies. There was none of the warm atmosphere that I had so much enjoyed in Geneva. The lunches I was forced to take at the hospital dining room were awful. There were, daily, marjoram potatoes and rotten peas – on some days a thin slice of dark bread as a delicacy was the only variety. The only good thing was that everyone was in the same boat, the same grinding poverty everywhere, and this facilitated a kind of bond. There was a very touching poster in all the street cars showing a well fed and politely smiling butcher cutting slices of sausage and asking the customer, "Could it be a little more, my lady?" and then, "If you wish to see this again, don't forget to turn off the gas faucet."

In my free time, I studied, preparing to take my remaining four exams in order to get my Viennese diploma. I also traveled to Lilienfeld (two hours by train) to see Bamer, who practiced there, and met his wife Rosi and their twin babies, and heard their sorrowful story of the war years and the miracle of their survival. Franz had contracted TB working in a sanitarium in northern Germany (where he met Rosi) and became deathly ill. At the end of the war, they fled and made their way south to Austria, because Rosi's home (her parents had a huge farm in eastern Prussia) had been taken over by the Russians. They were almost killed in an air raid on a train station during their travels, but they did make it to Vienna, from where Franz was sent to a TB sanitarium in Tirol, more dead than alive. Nobody expected him to survive, but he did, coming back after a year and starting a practice in Lilienfeld. Their first baby was stillborn – but they had eight after that! Kurt had sent them a care package which arrived at the very worst time and, as Rosi said, literally saved Franz's life when there was nothing to eat!

I also saw Wenger who had married a German girl and had come back right after the war to join the staff of the Department of Medicine at the University Clinic. It was nice to see these old friends, but otherwise everything was depressing, the grinding poverty and the ubiquitous evidence of a defeated and occupied country, with all the imposed restrictions on personal freedom. After working for three months at the clinic, I took my exams in September and passed them all with the exception of Hygiene. I had never flunked an examination before and it did upset me! I guess I had been too confident. In any case, I felt I had had it. Maybe if Trude had been around, and if I had not known there was another possibility (even though far in the future) – America, I might have stuck it out. Who knows? Was it the right decision? It certainly seemed so at first.

It was great to be back in Geneva with the family and the "meat pots of Egypt," modest as they were. When I went to

Franceschetti's clinic, he welcomed me warmly and mentioned that there might be a chance for me to get a job substituting for one of his assistants (Stadlin), who was going on a sabbatical for a year in Belgium. Before long I was really given this position and was now part of the clinic and very happy about it. In my whole life this year was by far the happiest because of the unique spirit that pervaded the clinic. I never worked as hard and with so much pleasure and excitement as then; and never again did I have so many ideas or write so many papers. Research seemed to be in the air and we all worked on some paper all the time. Usually once a week, the "patron," as Franceschetti was called, would ask everyone of us sitting around the big table in the library where we all met every morning: "What are you working on?" or "How are you coming with your paper?" He always took extra time to talk with us, usually in the evening to look over our papers again when we were ready to show them to him.

His Christmas parties were delightful! Everybody working at the clinic was invited and there were shows acting out funny scenes from the life in the clinic, humorous stories about happenings in anyone's professional life were told, often in the form of a poem. Everyone was given presents, distributed by the patron, and had to show them in front of everybody. A great deal of thought must have gone into selecting these presents, because they were very imaginative. I remember, for instance, that Dr. Bourquin, one of the assistants who was considered a retinal specialist and who prided himself on always finding the holes in cases of retinal detachment, even when others failed, got a huge piece of Swiss cheese with exceptionally numerous and large holes.

The year I invented my knife for lamellar corneal transplants (which applied the potato peeler principle to a corneal knife), my present was a beautiful high quality steel bread knife (which we still use) with an accompanying fictitious letter by

Sir Stewart Duke-Elder (the British king of ophthalmology), congratulating me on the invention of the "Couteau Bock." The letter also expressed the wish that I may always have plenty of bread to use the bread knife for. Franceschetti knew, of course, that I was very short of money and on one occasion, after I told him of Tinki's birth, he even gave me a check. I was very touched by his thoughtfulness, but even more by his gesture of letting me operate on one of the cataracts that morning, which was a very special privilege. I never cashed the check, but kept it for emergencies, and returned it to him when I left the clinic.

Meanwhile, Vater was getting ready to leave for Germany to take over a church sponsored project for resettlement of East German refugees near Frankfurt. They were starting with practically nothing on a hill overlooking Bad Vilbel, that had been an army training ground under the Nazis. It was the beginning of what was to become Heilsberg, and by the spring of 1948, the first two rows of houses were finished, one of which was to be the pastor's. Mutter was to follow him as soon as possible. It was a very hard and primitive life for Vater, I am sure, but there were the usual rewards of working with like-minded and dedicated people and of building something that was so obviously needed. For us, this meant that we had to find another place to live. Since Trude's US quota was open, because she had been born in Germany (the quota depended on the country of birth), she could get her immigration visa at any time, while mine was still up in the air. Moreover, we realized soon after Christmas that she was expecting again, so there was enough reason to consider seriously her going ahead to America to stay with Kurt, who had invited her to come. In this way, our next child would automatically be an American citizen.

It was not an easy decision to make, but in the end it seemed the most reasonable thing to do. We were so absolutely sure of each other that we did not worry too much about the emotional impact of a separation for an uncertain length of time. So Trude left by plane with Marianne at the beginning of March 1948, and I rented a small room at the "Bout du Monde" near the river Arve. My work at the clinic was so absorbing (in addition I took cello lessons) that the separation was not too hard, although I could not say that I liked it either. We kept in close contact by mail and Trude seemed to manage pretty well in her little cottage in Kurt's garden. I needed so little to live on that my small salary was enough to send Trude sufficient for her groceries and Kurt took care of the rest. So it was all a question of waiting and more waiting. That is what life consists of anyway, only one is not always as aware of it. Franceschetti tried to intervene with the US Consul in Zurich for me; and Kurt certainly did his share in pushing his congressman in order to expedite my visa, but there was no getting around the law. Not even the American daughter made a difference. It was hard to understand how anyone could make such stupid, inhuman laws. It was now over two years since I had applied for immigration in Peking and still no one could tell me when my quota might come up.

In the fall of 1949, the position of Assistant in the Eye Clinic of the Aarau County Hospital became available and, since my substituting job with Franceschatti came to an end with Dr. Stadlin's return, I took that opportunity to have an income. I moved, with a heavy heart, to Aarau. What a contrast! Not only professionally, but in the whole climate. To me, Geneva was the large, but still intimate, clinic full of vitality and excitement, the comradeship with the other assistants, the sharing of all interesting things that were going on, the warmth of the patron and the general charm, wit and light-heartedness of the French character. It was cosmopolitan with the many visiting ophthalmologists from all over Europe and the numerous foreign patients that Franceschetti's fame had attracted. All this made it such a pleasant place to be.

In Aarau, the outlook on life was very provincial, stoic, slow and pedantic. I had to take care of many more patients all by myself and my Chief, Dr. Knuesel, was, in his reserved German/Swiss way, just the opposite of Franceschetti. He was about to retire and did not show much interest in.the large clinic (we had about fifty eye beds). He never once invited me to his house; neither had he ever invited my predecessor, Dr. Kurz, in the nine years they had worked together. Dr. Kurz was now about to leave for Israel and did not have much time or patience to break me in. This did not matter too much, because the nurses were all very nice (Emma, Margarit, Trudy), and helped me all they could to make the transition easier. We are still corresponding with Nurse Trudy in St. Gallen. She is one of those friends for life, like one finds in the German part of Switzerland. It takes awhile to make friends, but once this has happened, it is there for good. We were very busy and I saw a lot of interesting pathology and surgery. Dr. Knuesel did give me permission to travel to Geneva every two or three weeks on weekends to keep in touch with the clinic there. I could afford these trips now because my salary was substantially more than it had been in Geneva. I rented a room next to the hospital and took my meals at the hospital.

The wooded hills around Aarau are very nice and in my spare time, I took up mushroom hunting again with Dr. Othmar Weihs, the radiologist who became a good and devoted friend. He was a very gentle man who had come some fifteen years ago from Austria, because he had married a Swiss physician who was now in charge of the X-ray Department while he did the radiotherapy. However, he had never been given Swiss citizenship and, accordingly, although he did the work of a physician, was officially only his wife's assistant and was paid as an X-ray technician. This was an example of how impossible the Swiss made it for foreigners to really settle in their country. They had helped innumerable people during the war, but there was a limit to the number of refugees they would take in. During the war, they made it extremely tough for people to come in. Those who did manage to get across, got only very limited permission to stay and were constantly reminded to leave as soon as possible. To be fair, I must mention however, at least one true story. After the Nazi invasion of France, two children were brought to Vater's office at the World Council of Churches in Geneva. They had fled across the border in the Jura mountains. Their only identification was a label tied around their neck with the name Freudenberg on it, and the border guards let them pass, apparently because they knew him from his refugee work!

I was closer now to the US Embassy in Zurich and made more frequent calls there to find out about my quota, but it was always the same answer, "We have no idea when yours will come, since quota numbers are distributed on a world wide basis from Washington. Yours has not arrived." So, by summer of 1949, after a year and a half of separation, we decided that this was too long and uncertain a wait and that Trude should come back. She arrived by ship in Genoa, where I picked them up and made the acquaintance of my second daughter, who was then one year old and impressed me as a fat little babe that felt very much at home the moment she was put in the bath tub at the hotel. Marianne had grown a lot and was a cute little girly. They both had a very uninhibited natural way – quite different from the usual European child at that time. We went to the family chalet in Champex Switzerland first, where the grandparents were waiting for us, and then I went on to Aarau to fix up our little flat above the chicken coop in a farm house nearby in Buchs. It was a tiny attic apartment, consisting of only one room, a kitchen and a toilet, but its great advantage was that our very nice neighbor, Mrs. Mueller, was an ideal helper for Trude. Trude managed amazingly well under the rather primitive circumstances, never complaining, and we were happy to be together again. In the following Spring, I went to Austria to make another try at passing my examination in Hygiene, and this time I made it and got my Viennese doctor's diploma in due course. I also obtained a certificate as a specialist in ophthalmology and was now all set to practice in Austria. This was a good psychological antidote against the frustration that was building up about the US immigration quota and my mind began to explore more and more the idea of actually returning to Austria. Both Bamer and Wenger encouraged me very much, but I knew that Trude did not like the idea. To her, Austria was a strange country where she felt acutely uncomfortable with her German accent and the peculiar friendliness of the people. She disliked the Austrians as much as the Germans and had an almost paranoid fear of being taken in Austria for a Nazi, thereby being either loved by former collaborators or hated by former patriotic Austrians. She liked the scenic beauty, but never had any warm feelings for the people. I guess this must have been some unconscious residual from the times of Frederick the Great of Prussia!

With me it was just the opposite. Whenever I was there for a few days, my dialect came back and everything brought back mostly good memories that made me feel at home. I don't know why I didn't harbor more of a grudge against the people. Many of them had done all those horrible things to us, but I associated mostly, of course, with old and proven friends and I could see how the people had all suffered a great deal from this tragic, insane movement and the war.

On one occasion while visiting friends in Austria, I had the strong wish to see "our" Attersee again, even if only for a brief moment. I felt particularly keen on visiting Bruggraben Klamm at the south shore of the lake. It is a spectacular narrow, rocky gorge that one follows on a kind of trail. It is mostly steps in an almost vertical rock wall, where one walks along, while holding on to a cable for dear life. Below is the cascading creek, and after about twenty-five minutes of walking, a high waterfall blocks further progress. As children, we had done this trail many times because it was so exciting. In the woods, just before entering the gorge itself, there was a little shrine with a statue of Mary, and way above (almost hidden by trees) a crucifix. There were always little candles burning there that one could buy for a few cents and then light. On this particular visit, I went up to this natural shrine and did just that. To my surprise, I discovered a small three-by-six-inch bronze plaque solidly attached to the rock. I did not remember having seen this here before. The short inscription read "Den Verstorbenen Heimat Vertriebenen." I could not believe my eyes (because of tears). To translate these 4 words into English takes a whole sentence – "In memory of those who were driven from their home country and died in foreign lands." How could I not feel addressed by this very personal message. This one com-passionate understanding sentence from some Austrian heart wiped out whatever resentment I still might have harbored against my former home country.

Sometime in the fall of 1950, I went back to Austria with the idea of finding a place to practice in Salzburg. A former classmate, Dr. Hroch, practiced in the city of Salzburg and suggested that I try somewhere else nearby. I investigated Schwarzach-St. Veit, a little town in the Salzach Valley, important only as a railroad center and because of a fair sized hospital. The chief surgeon was very encouraging, and I liked the scenery (Trude thought it was terrible because it was completely closed in by high mountains). I found a nice little house suitable for both home and practice and made a down payment on the rent so they would hold it for us until Trude would have a chance to see it. When I came back to Aarau with this news, Trude was naturally not too enthusiastic. She could not see herself being stuck in a mountain village in an undesirable country with no chance for development. So we debated back and forth, Kurt from America also expressing his regret at the idea and hoping that we would wait it out to go to America where the chances for a "good life" seemed so much better. Eventually, I decided to try Austria once more – something was pulling me back – and I guess I was also apprehensive of the struggle and the strangeness that awaited me in America.

But it was not to happen. Shortly after we had finally agreed to make the move to Austria, the US Embassy informed me of the arrival of my quota. So we were back with the old dilemma, and this time Trude won out and convinced me that America was the way to go. The year and a half in Berkeley had made her aware of the good side of the country with its freedom, generosity, openmindedness – and also the material amenities – so there was no doubt in *her* mind, particularly considering the future of the children.

Mama made her first visit to Austria just about the time we left Aarau, and she dropped in on us the day we left. My good friend, Peter Sachs , whom I had come to know and like on his visits to our hospital as a detail man for CIBA, gave us a warm farewell in Basel. We had talked much in the past about our dilemma – America versus Austria – and he, knowing my non-aggressive nature, had always felt that America was not the country for me, so all he could do was wish me good luck and warn me that "honesty was not a Swiss export article," as he expressed it.

Paris, which could have been interesting, was instead a week of chasing back and forth to the US Embassy because Marianne, who had left the US on Trude's passport, did not have any reentry papers and they had to be procured in a hurry. Tinki was all right because of her famous US birth certificate. Still, we found some time to visit with the Ostrovskys who had settled in Paris, and Father Teilhard de Chardin. We also visited the Louvre once for a whole morning (great) and saw Notre Dame, the Sainte Chapel and the quai at the Quartier Latin. I had never seen such beautiful stained glass windows. Also we saw the Dome des Invalides with Napoleon's tomb, the Arc de Triomphe and the Eiffel Tower, because most of these sites were within walking distance of our hotel. We had been advised to see the UNRRA officials in Paris and were glad that we did, because it turned out that they would pay for our transportation to the US. This was a big break, because we just had enough money for our fare to New York and had planned to borrow from Kurt for our beginning. Now we felt very rich and secure!

America The Beautiful

We boarded the *SS America* in Le Havre and stopped for four days in Southampton, which gave me a chance to see a little of London, where Trude's Uncle Walter and grandmother were staying. He was just visiting from Israel. Arrival in New York (March 6, 1951) was exciting. As we sailed along the coast of Long Island, I could see the cars on the freeways driving at what seemed an incredible speed. I got scared just looking at them and could not imagine ever driving that fast myself. I had taken driving lessons in Switzerland, but did not do too well, so this first sight of America was not exactly encouraging! But the Statue of Liberty was something else again! She is not a beauty but is impressive in her size and touching in what she expresses. How many millions must have looked at her with tears in their eyes when they first came to this country.

Some of Vater's "refugee" clients had found a hotel for us, but I shipped Trude and the girls off to California as soon as possible. I knew they were better off in Kurt's garden cottage while I was: making my initial professional contacts, applying for first papers, and taking English and Medical State Board license exams (which I found I could already take in June). I took the train to Baltimore to see Dr. Friedenwald at Johns Hopkins, with whom Dr. Franceschetti had corresponded about me. I had hoped to get a research job there. I am amazed at the confidence I showed, which was only possible because I had been completely unaware of the caliber of ophthalmology practiced in that department. I even showed my little movie with the "Bock knife" for lamellar kerotoplasty. I also visited the Presbyterian Hospital in New York, but didn't have a chance for a job there either, of course. At the beginning of

April I left for the west coast, after I had arranged to take part in a crash preparatory course for the board exams in New York. I stopped in Ann Arbor to see Lislott and to meet her surgeon husband, Bill Coon, and then I went on to California to see the rest of the family in Berkeley. These were happy days to see them all again, after so many years of separation. Trude and the kids had settled right back into their familiar surroundings and I was glad to see them so well taken care of.

I visited Stanford to call on Dr. Maumenee, who was just then looking for a researcher in his corneal transplant work. This was exactly what I wanted and it was then that I thought for the first time that it had been a good idea to come to America. Kurt had written to me in Europe already about the fabulous Lake Tahoe that he had recently discovered. So, in celebration of these happy events, the two of us drove up there to see it and, possibly, to find a small house to buy. He felt that with two families to use it, it wasn't such a luxury. It was early in the season and there was a lot of snow on the mountains, which made it all the more beautiful. We took a crosscountry hike up to Marlette Lake, and on coming down, I must have twisted my back, because I developed sciatic pains on the left side the next day – the beginning of my disc troubles.

Returning to New York, I really buckled down on my preparation for the State Board Exams. The daily three hour intensive course given by a German refugee doctor in his office was excellent and I could not have done without it. The room I rented was near City College, so I could go down to Central Park and sit there studying on a bench on good days. Occasionally, I took the subway out to the Cloisters to work there in the beautiful park. Otherwise, I made no attempts to get to know New York better. It did not interest me and I was too busy trying to cover and absorb the vast amount of medical knowledge that was expected of us in the exams less than three months hence. Whatever I could not avoid seeing of New York, otherwise, made me dislike it as a big city. It did not help that Dr. Falkenstein, a former "client" of Vater's and an old misanthrope German refugee doctor, who practiced on the next block from where I lived, misdiagnosed my sciatic pains as caused by diabetes. The laboratory he sent me to for a glucose tolerance test apparently was not too reliable, so I had to learn to live with this not very pleasant thought of being diabetic. This scepter haunted me for many years to come and I am still mad at this old fool who certainly was not the greatest of healers.

In the beginning of June, I passed my English language examination and then, toward the end of June, I took the medical board exam. The closer I came to the exams, the less I could face all my books. I developed a sense of mental nausea, a sensation as if it were impossible to cram any more into this poor brain of mine. The evening of the last examination day, I jumped on the train to California, relieved that this phase of my life was over. Somehow, I also had the feeling that I had passed the test. On July 1, I started my research job at Stanford and on the 7th, Michael was born. By now we were five and the friendly little cottage in Kurt's garden with its two rooms really had become too small. It had been quite crowded with only Trude and the girls there. We had been taking walks through the neighboring streets, looking out for places to rent – mysteriously attracted more to old houses, as in Europe. On one of these walks we went all the way up to the beautiful rose garden. We did not find an apartment or house, but the exercise was apparently so stimulating that Michael was born that same night. Eventually, we found a two room apartment on Dwight Way and settled in happily. Kurt had been very helpful all along and enjoyed it when he could show us the beauty of the Bay Area which he had come to love so much. He gave me driving lessons and eventually turned Felicia's old

Pontiac over to me so that I could commute to my job.

On our frequent walks in the neighborhood, we discovered the old Unitarian Church next to the UC campus, a charming wooden building, darkened by age and overgrown with ivy – so unlike most of the churches here. We had been made aware of the Unitarians by Pfarrer Oser in Aarau, whose liberal sermons we had often enjoyed, so we tried going there to see what it was all about. The minister, Rev. Cope, was a very interesting, philosophically minded man whom we liked very much. He introduced us to the denomination and we felt quite happy in their humanistic, idealistic and rationalistic outlook on life. Later, in San Francisco, we joined the church there and enjoyed Rev. Meserve at least as much, although he was suffering through a divorce at the time. The San Francisco church was an old gothic style stone building, very much like the European churches, giving me a little of the feeling of home. I still remember the quote from Micah over one of the windows, "What does the Lord require of thee but to do justice, to love mercy and to walk humbly with thy God."

When we eventually moved to Palo Alto, we joined the church here. Our minister was Dan Lion, a very straight New Englander, and in the course of time, we met a number of nice people who became permanent friends . Later on I even taught Sunday School and took on the job of West Coast Representative of the Unitarian Service Committee, under whose auspices I went to India in 1960. But somehow, I got tired and disillusioned with the overemphasis on the human element in this brand of religion, which at times smacked a little too much of conceit. Also, the church itself changed more toward political radicalism, which left me cold. Our association with this group of idealistic people has done a great deal in helping us to assimilate with and understand some of the best traditions of this country, but we slowly drifted away.

My research project consisted of studying the immune

reaction that led to graft rejection. I found myself very poorly prepared for this work and not too clever in making up for my deficiencies by reading in the library. What bothered me more and more was to have to torture those poor rabbits on whom the operations were performed – and after a few months, I realized that I really was not made for research. Anyway, I did conceive the idea of using interlamellar grafts for experimental work, which proved a very useful method for research in this field. No paper of any significance came of all this work, but as Kurt said, what was really important for me was the contacts and connections I had made during the year. They helped me to make a start in a new country.

We had to decide whether I wanted to return to New York to practice there (I had passed my boards and was, therefore, entitled to open shop there) or try to stay in California where a year of internship and repeating the California board examination was required for the license to practice. By some quaint lucky circumstance, I did not have to be a US citizen, which was normally a prerequisite to taking the boards here. For once a stupid law was in my favor! Because I had an MD degree from China where US physicians were allowed to practice without a license, California allowed me by reciprocity, to take the exams without being a citizen. It was a hard decision, nevertheless. I knew that Kurt and Mama wanted me to stay, of course, but Kurt did not try to influence me except by offering us a loan if I should decide to go through the internship here, which did not pay enough to live on. After long deliberation, and knowing that Trude also liked it here much better, I decided to put in another year and study again for the boards.

In July 1952, 1 started my internship at the SP Hospital in San Francisco and we moved to a third-floor, somewhat larger, apartment two blocks from the hospital. It was not a bad year, certainly much less strenuous than the Peking internship, and

I learned a lot. Much was new in medicine since I'd taken my last practical year, ten years ago. Trude worked hard with taking care of the children. The worst for her was to lug Michael up and down those stairs. He was a very heavy baby and refused to walk for way too long. He preferred to slide around on his bottom, often with lightning speed.

On Sundays they were all allowed to come to the hospital dining room for lunch or dinner, where there was the opportunity to meet other young couples with children and give Trude a little reprieve from the kitchen. The year passed very quickly and another examination with its preparation was drawing closer. I also began to look around for a place to practice and made connections with Dr. Poore in Palo Alto, who promised to take me in after I got my boards. In June, Trude and the kids moved up to Tahoe to live in Kurt's cabin in Kings Beach where it was much nicer for them, and we also could save rent money for the summer months until I knew where we would settle. I joined them after the board exams in July and waited for the results there. The trouble was that, while I waited, Dr. Poore took in another associate, so I was left high and dry and disappointed in my Palo Alto plans. Somehow, though, I had set my mind on this town and when, finally, the positive answer from the board exams came in September, I set out to start my office here on Forest Street, just around the corner from Dr. Poore's office. I rented a simple house on Addison Street and the family moved down at the end of September.

It was exciting to start my own practice, even though it was very slow and I had plenty of time to practice my cello at the office while waiting for patients. I have never been any good at drumming up business, but Dr. Smith, who was about to retire and, occasionally also, Dr. Poore, sent me some of their patients. Since patience has always been one of my stronger characteristics, we stuck it out. Actually, I had much more surgery the first year in practice than I have now, with our area so oversaturated with superspecialists.

Trude liked the Addison house because of its simplicity and the large wild backyard, and we were happy there. I joined Henry Holt's symphonietta where I met Anita Barrett and Barbara, whose husband got me to join the Sierra Club. In June 1954, Oliver made his appearance, and I made the discovery of the Sierra Nevada on my first knapsack trip with the Sierra Club. Having found the mountains again was a very important factor in getting acclimated to this country. About that same time, borrowing a $5,000 down payment from Kurt, we bought the Hamilton house and settled in.

Postscript: December 1999

Reading this story twenty-two years after I wrote it makes me feel even more aware of how privileged I was to have survived those dangerous years – how a benevolent guiding hand must have held me up all along. This explains the new title: "Gratefully Looking Back – A Doctor's Special Journey," which also seems more fitting and in line with my maturing religious outlook on life. The miracle of my survival – while millions of innocent people perished – is the main story. But it did not end there. Allowing me to develop secure roots again here in America made me aware of what I really owe to this country. I had seen so much poor medical care in developing countries – why couldn't I apply my knowledge by volunteering from time to time overseas, as a way to say "thank you" to America! I started with India in 1960, followed by a dozen other countries over the years. They were all fascinating, moving experiences that I enjoyed writing about. The American Academy of Ophthalmology in San Francisco is keeping these reports in their Archives.

Appendix

Deutsche Botschaft
Dienststelle
DR 3-2c/5824/42

Herrn Dr. Rudolf Israel Bock, geboren am
20.April 1915 in Wien wird hiermit bescheingt,
dass ihm laut Bekanntmachung im Reichsgesetz-
blatt Teil I Nr. 133 vom 26.November k941 die
deutsche Staatsangehoerigkeit aberkannt worden
ist.
    Demzufolge ist von ihm der Deutsche Reise-
pass Nr. 180 ausgestellt am 12.September 1938
vom Polizeikommissariat Wiener-Neustadt einge-
zogen worden.
    Eine chinesische Uebersetzung der Beschei-
nigung befindet sich auf der Rueckseite,Licht-
bild und Unterschrift befinden sich hierneben.

            Peking, dem 14.Dezember 1942

            DEUTSCHE BOTSCHAFT
            Dienststelle
                I.A.

                Hornemann.

Revocation of German Citizenship – in German

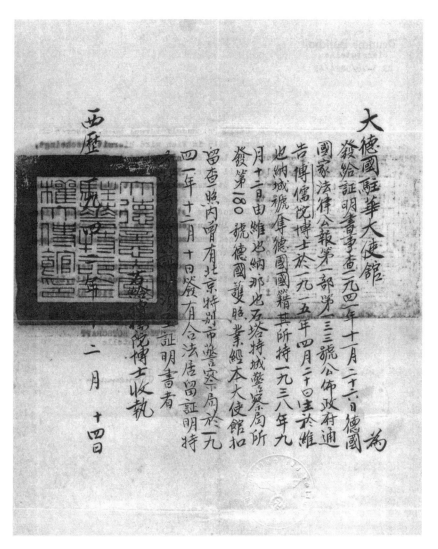

大德國駐華大使館

為

發給証明書事查二九四一年十一月二十六日德國

國家法律公報第一部第一三三號公佈政府通

告傅儒汜博士於一九二五年四月二十四日生於維

也納城根傳德國國籍其所持一九三八年九

月十二日由維也納那屯石塔特城警察局所

發第180號德國護照業經本大使館扣

留查照內曾有北京特別市警察局於一九

四一年十二月十日發有合法居留証特

此証明書者

西歷

一九四二年

……博士收執

二月 十四

Revocation of German Citizenship - in Chinese

DEKANAT
DER
MEDIZINISCHEN FAKULTÄT
DER UNIVERSITÄT IN WIEN

WIEN, am 18.November 1938.

Zahl 401 aus 19 38/39.

Herrn

Rudolf B o c k

Wr. Neu s t a d t

Bahngasse 2.

Auf Ihre an das Ministerium gerich-
tete Eingabe wird Ihnen seitens des medizinischen Dekanates mitge-
teilt,dasz Sie im Sinne der Anordnung des Reichserziehungsministers,
Zahl 57, Berlin W/8/36/34/11/2122 vom 11.November 1938 bis auf Wei-
teres keine Prüfungen ablegen können.

Der kommissarische Dekan:

Denial of permission to complete medical studies by the
University of Vienna November 18, 1938.

Der Reichsminifter
für Wiffenfchaft, Erziehung
und Volksbildung

Berlin W 8, den   15. Dezember 1938.
Unter den Linden 69

Fernfprecher: 11 00 30
Poftfcheckkonto: Berlin 144 0t
Reichsbank=Giro=konto
Poftfach

-WP Nr. 3355-

Es wird gebeten, diefes Gefchäftszeichen und den
Gegenftand bei weiteren Schreiben anzugeben.

Zum Schreiben vom 24. November 1938 betr. Studium der Medizin an der Universität in Wien.

Ihrer Bitte, das Studium der Medizin an der Universität in Wien beenden zu dürfen, habe ich nicht entsprechen können.

Im Auftrage
gez. Bach.

Beglaubigt.

Derwaltungsfekretär.

An
Herrn Rudolf Bock

Wiener Neustadt,

Bahngasse 2.

Denial of permission to complete medical studies by the
Ministry of Education December 15, *1938*.

院學醫和協平北立私

PEIPING UNION MEDICAL COLLEGE

部 書 註
OFFICE OF THE RECORDER

February 28, 1939.

Dear Mr. Book:

Your letter of February 23rd addressed to Dr. Hsien Wu, Chairman of our Committee on Admissions has been referred to the Dean's Office for further attention. The Committee is prepared to accept your gymnasium qualification in lieu of our entrance examination for admission to our medical college as a special case. Your attention is drawn to page 37 of our Announcement, sent you under separate cover.

For advanced standing in the medical college you will be required to pass all the examinations in which exemption from our courses is sought as stipulated in our Announcement in page 38 under "d. Pass examinations given by the departments concerned in the subjects in which advanced standing is desired." Please note that we cannot grant you exemption from examination in any of the subjects. Our regulations are inflexible in this respect and we wish to draw your attention to them before your coming to us.

Should you come here you will, therefore, have to take first our examinations in Anatomy, Biochemistry, Physiology, Pharmacology, Bacteriology and Pathology including Parasitology. After passing all these examinations you may then take the examination in Chinese in September according to our regulations in page 42, section 3 "No student may take a clinical clerkship with unfinished work in anatomy, physiology, biochemistry, pharmacology, pathology, or bacteriology; or without a satisfactory knowledge of spoken mandarin Chinese." In case of failure in any of the subjects you will be required to repeat the course and it is only after satisfactory passing of all the subjects listed above that you will be allowed to take examinations and courses in the clinical subjects.

In addition we wish to point out that students are required to live in our Students Dormitory where only Chinese food is provided. Furthermore, you will be required to pass a complete medical examination given by the College Physician, as mentioned in page 36, section D.

If there are any other points that are not clear to you please do not hesitate to ask for further information before you make decision to come here.

Yours sincerely,

Dean of the Medical College

Mr. Rudolf H. Book
c/o Mr. Paul Patek,
907, Higashi 2-chome,
Magomemachi, Omori-ku
Tokyo, Japan.

CEL:PkC.

Letter of acceptance to Peking University, February 1939

Doctor of Medicine diploma, Peking Union Medical
College - 1941